ThailandCONDENSED

ThailandCONDENSED

2000 years of history and culture

Ellen London

Marshall Cavendish
Editions

Series Editor: Melvin Neo
Designer: Lynn Chin Nyuk Ling

Published by Marshall Cavendish Editions
An imprint of Marshall Cavendish International
1 New Industrial Road, Singapore 536196

Other Marshall Cavendish Offices:
Marshall Cavendish Ltd. 5th Floor, 32-38 Saffron Hill, London EC1N 8FH, UK • Marshall Cavendish Corporation. 99 White Plains Road, Tarrytown NY 10591-9001, USA • Marshall Cavendish International (Thailand) Co Ltd. 253 Asoke, 12th Flr, Sukhumvit 21 Road, Klongtoey Nua, Wattana, Bangkok 10110, Thailand • Marshall Cavendish (Malaysia) Sdn Bhd, Times Subang, Lot 46, Subang Hi-Tech Industrial Park, Batu Tiga, 40000 Shah Alam, Selangor Darul Ehsan, Malaysia

Marshall Cavendish is a trademark of Times Publishing Limited

National Library Board Singapore Cataloguing in Publication Data

London, Ellen.
Thailand condensed : 2000 years of history and culture / Ellen London. – Singapore : Marshall Cavendish Editions, c2008.
p. cm.
Includes bibliographical references and index.
ISBN-13 : 978-981-261-520-6 (pbk.)
ISBN-10 : 981-261-520-2 (pbk.)

1. Thailand – History. 2. Thailand – Civilization. I. Title.

DS571
959.3—dc22   OCN191792624

Printed in Singapore by Times Graphics Pte Ltd

PREFACE

Thailand is a fascinating and beautiful country with an interesting and diverse history. The Thai people inhabit regions as varied as the coastlines, lowland valleys and mountainous north; the country consists of large urban centres as well as remote rural villages.

Bordered by Burma to the south and southwest, Laos to the north and east, Cambodia to the southeast and Malaysia to the south, Thai history and culture bears the influences of these neighbouring countries. At the same time, modern Thailand is represented by a rich tapestry of creative arts (music, dance, art and architecture), literature and handicrafts that are unique and quintessentially Thai. The golden stitches holding the tapestry together are undoubtedly those of the spiritual, particularly the Buddhist religion.

Research and information in the writing of this book was gleaned from a variety of reliable print and electronic reference resources, as well as through discussions with professionals and experts in Thailand. Thailand Condensed presents Thailand from its earliest days to the present. It is not intended to be a comprehensive, in-depth academic publication, but an easily readable text presenting the reader with a broad spectrum of interesting facts and information about the country.

CONTENTS

CONTENTS

CHRONOLOG

HISTORICAL HIGHLIGHTS

13th century   First Tai kingdoms established

                  Tais have extensive settlements in Chao Phraya Basin

                  Sukothai Kingdom established (Ramkhamhaeng 1279–98)

                  Stone inscription of earliest representations of
                      Thai language

                  Lan Na established; capital of Chiang Mai established

15th century   Tais drive Khmers from Ayutthaya and overthrow
                      capital at Angkor

                  Sukothai becomes a province of Ayutthaya

15th-17th century European missionaries and traders come to Siam

                  Siam closes doors to Europeans

16th century   Myanmar triumphs and takes control of Lan Na

18th century	Ayutthaya destroyed by Myanmar forces (1767)
	Thon Buri becomes new capital of Siam (1767)
	Trade with China encouraged
	Revolt of Lan Na (1771–74)

19th century	Lan Na under Tai control
	Bangkok becomes capital of Siam
	Burney Treaty between Siam and Britain (1826)
	Bowring Treaty (1855)
	First Bangkok newspaper (1844)
	Thai Baht currency introduced (1897)
	Rama V surrenders Siam's Lao territories to France
	Britain takes over rights of four Malay States from Siam

20th century	Mandatory primary education & understanding Thai language & principles
	Mandatory for Thais to have a surname (1913)
	Coup of 1932
	Name of country changed from Siam to Thailand (1939)
	Thailand gains control over French Territories in Laos and northwestern Cambodia (1940)
	Treaty of Alliance between Thailand and Japan; Thailand declares war on Britain and the US (1942)
	Thailand becomes charter member of Southeast Asia Treaty Organisation (1954)

Thailand sends troops in alliance with the United States in Vietnam War (1964–69)

Massive demonstrations in Bangkok demanding proclamation of a Constitution (1973)

Vietnam occupies Cambodia (1979); refugees entering Thailand

Asian Currency Crisis (1997)

21st century   Avian influenza in Thailand (2003)

First human deaths from avian influenza (2004)

Indian Ocean tsunami (2004)

State of Emergency declared (2005)

CHAKRI DYNASTY (Bangkok Kings)

1. Rama I (Phra Phutthayotfa)	6 Apr 1782 – 7 Sep 1809
2. Rama II (Phra Phutthaloetla)	7 Sep 1809 – 21 Jul 1824
3. Rama III (Phra Nangklao)	21 Jul 1824 – 3 Apr 1851
4. Rama IV (Mongkut)	3 Apr 1851 – 1 Oct 1868
5. Rama V (Chulalongkorn)	1 Oct 1868 – 23 Oct 1910
6. Rama VI (Vajiravudh)	23 Oct 1910 – 26 Nov 1925
7. Rama VII (Prajadhipok)	26 Nov 1925 – 2 Mar 1935 [abdicated]
8. Rama VIII (Ananda Mahidol)	2 Mar 1935 – 9 Jun 1946
9. Rama IX (Bhumibol Adulyadej)	9 Jun 1946 – present

KINGS OF AYUTTHAYA

1. Ramathibodi	1351–1369
2. Ramesuan	1369–1370
3. Borommaracha I	1370–1388
4. Thong Chan	1388
5. Ramesuan (second)	1388–1395
6. Ramaracha	1395–1409
7. Intharacha	1409–1424
8. Borommaracha II	1424–1448
9. Borommatrailokanat	
— Ayutthaya	1448–1463
— Phitsanulok	1463–1488
10. Borommaracha III (Ayutthaya)	1463–1488
11. Intharacha II (same person as #10)	1488–1491
12. Ramathibodi II	1491–1529
13. Borommaracha IV	1529–1533
14. Ratsada	1533–1534
15. Chairacha	1534–1547
16. Yot Fa	1547–1548
17. Khun Worawongsa	1548
18. Chakkraphat	1548–1569
19. Mahin	1569
20. Maha Thammaracha	1569–1590
21. Naresuan	1590–1605
22. Ekathotsarot	1605–1610/11

23. Si Saowaphak	1610–1611
24. Song Tham (Intharacha)	1610–1628
25. Chettha	1628–1629
26. Athittayawong	1629
27. Prasat Thong	1629–1656
28. Chai	1 day in August 1656
29. Suthammaracha	3 months 1656
30. Narai	1656–1688
31. Phra Phetracha	1688–1703
32. Sua	1703–1709
33. Phumintharacha (Thai Sa)	1709–1733
34. Boronmakot	1733–1758
35. Uthumphon	1 month 1758
36. Suriyamarin	1758–1767

KINGS OF LAN NA

1. Mangrai	1259–1317
2. Cheyyasongkhram	1317–1318
3. Saen Phu	1318–1319
4. Khrua	1319–1322
5. Nam Thuam	1322–1324
6. Saen Phu (second)	1324–1328
7. Kham Fu	1328–1337
8. Pha Yu	1345–1355

29. Chephutarai (Burmese)	1675–1707
30. Mangraenara (Burmese)	1707–1727
31. Thep Sing	1727
32. Ong Kham	1727–1759
33. Chan	1759–1761
34. Khi Hut	1761–1762
35. Abhayagamani (Burmese)	1766–1768
36. Moyagamani (Burmese)	1768–1771

KINGS OF SUKHOTHAI

1. Sri Indraditya	1239–1259
2. Ban Muang	1259–1279
3. Ramkhamhaeng	1279–1298
4. Lo hai	1298–1346/7
5. Ngua Nam Thom	1346–1347
6. Mahathammaracha I (Luthai)	1347/7–1368/74
7. Mahathammaracha II	1368/74–1398
8. Mahathammaracha III (Sai Luthai)	1398–1419
9. Mahathammaracha IV	1419–1438

MAP OF THAILAND

HISTORY

BACKGROUND

A Creation Myth

Thai folklore has it that a long time ago, a very poor brother and sister caught a bamboo rat that was burrowing in the earth. The rat told them a great flood was coming and advised them to seal themselves inside a large hollowed-out gourd until the floodwaters receded.

After the flood, the brother and sister realised that they were the only ones left alive. They received a "sign" from the heavens, and some time later the sister gave birth to a gourd. One day, hearing noises from the gourd, they opened it and people of all colours emerged from the gourd. This, so legend goes, is the origin of the various races and cultures in the Southeast Asian region.

Tai Cultural Identity

Historically, the Thai people are descended from speakers of a closely related family of languages known as Tai. Tai speakers share a collective linguistic and cultural identity. Although spread across different Southeast Asian countries, culturally they have much more in common with other Tai peoples than with other races of the same nationalities. In considering the very early history of Thailand, therefore, instead of looking only within the geographical boundaries of modern Thailand itself, we must examine the Tai peoples, languages and culture across mainland Southeast Asia.

Historians believe that the Tai peoples originated in northern Vietnam or China and gradually settled throughout Southeast Asia, arriving about 1,000 years ago in what is now Thailand. Thai people today belong to any one or a combination of the following groups: late-arriving Tai peoples, earlier Mon or Khmer peoples, Chinese or Indian immigrants, or other peoples. Indigenous peoples also form part of the evolution fabric of the Thai culture. Tai peoples in Southeast Asia today number an estimated total of 80–100 million. Of these, the largest group (approximately 35–40 million) lives in Thailand. Others who speak related languages and consider themselves part of the Tai ethnic and linguistic grouping include the Lao, Shan, Lu, Black Tai, Zhung, Nung and other groups. They live in Laos, Vietnam, Myanmar (Burma) and southwestern China.

ANCIENT HISTORY

Archaeological finds suggest that the geographical area now known as Thailand has been inhabited since prehistoric times, between 1 million and 500,000 years ago. Between 20,000 and 10,000 years ago, groups of hunters and gatherers lived in the land, probably using primitive versions of tools seen in rural Southeast Asia today. Other tools and weapons included bows and arrows, the blowpipe and rudimentary animal and fish traps. Agriculture and animal domestication may have begun about 12,000 years ago. According to archaeological finds in northeastern Thailand, copper and bronze working was established more than 5,000 years ago. Iron working and pottery date from about 3,000 years ago.

Modern scholars think the Tai peoples originated in northern Vietnam or China and had settled throughout Southeast Asia by the 8th century. They lived in small villages, fishing, practising subsistence rice farming and gathering food from the forest. Some trade existed, probably for textiles, tools and pottery. An animistic peoples, they believed in spirits that had to be appeased through offerings, prayers and ceremonies.

Tai Villages and Muang

Tai peoples lived in the lowlands and river valleys of mainland Southeast Asia. Assorted ethnic and linguistic groups lived in the hills. The Tai village consisted of nuclear families working as subsistence rice farmers, living in small houses elevated above the ground. Households bonded together for protection from external attacks and to share the burden of communal repairs and maintenance. Within the village, a council of elders was created to help settle problems, organise festivals and rites and manage the village. Villages would combine to form a *muang*, a group of villages governed by a *chao* (lord). Besides overseeing the villages, the lord also managed the hill groups who worked as slaves or labourers in the *muang*. It was convenient for a small village unit to be part of the larger *muang* unit in order to negotiate and deal effectively with the Vietnamese and Chinese. These foreign authorities acknowledged the *muang* and the Tai lords.

As a political unit, the *muang* were also able to negotiate internal disputes and dole out punishments as appropriate. Villagers paid taxes to the *muang*, enabling a relatively high standard of living within the *muang*. The *chao* usually appointed his eldest son heir to his position. There was always a shortage of labour in Tai villages. To some extent the *muang* was able to manage labour more effectively than if individual farms and villages had been left to coordinate it themselves. Interactions and relationships among the Tai, at the family, village and *muang* levels, as well as between the Tai and their labourers, were crucial. The *muang* organisational hierarchy functioned very effectively and efficiently.

Tai Expansion

One of the lord's goals was continually to expand his *muang* by conquering *muang* in other areas. To this end, he organised his men into a military group, typically led by his sons. Once a region was defeated, the *muang* lord settled families from the old *muang* into the newly conquered one. The new settlers' responsibility was to create rice fields from the forests they tamed. The lord's sons ruled the new communities. In this way, not only did the son have a position of power, the system also served to reinforce and extend the power of the 'parent' *muang*.

Scholars are divided about the origin of and territories occupied by the Tai peoples before the 8th century. The Lao origin legend of Khun Borom, retold by Wyatt in *Thailand: A Short History*, has it that after a great flood that wiped out everyone except three kings, the Tai peoples emerged from gourds to repopulate the earth.

The gods taught the Tai peoples how to build houses and to live according to a code of conduct, abiding by certain customs and rituals. As the populations increased, they spread over an area that included Luang Prabang, Siang Khwang, Ayutthaya, Chiang Mai, the Sipsong Pan Na (southern Yunnan), Hamsavati (the Mon state of Pegu in lower Burma) and a region in north-central Vietnam. Some scholars believe that between the 7th and 11th centuries, a geographical distribution of the Tai peoples existed that actually concurred with the diaspora described in this legend. More recent scholarship, however, traces the Tai homeland to an area that is now northern Vietnam.

Whatever the origin of the Tai peoples, they were living in northern Southeast Asia by the 8th century. Five linguistic groups emerged: the northern Tai in China (ancestors of the Zhuang); the upland Tai people in northern Vietnam (ancestors of the Black, White and Red Tai); the Tai in northeastern Laos and bordering Vietnam (ancestors of the Tai of Siang Khwang and the Siamese in Ayutthaya); the Tai in northern Laos; and the Tai west of Luang Prabang, northern Thailand and in the adjoining parts of Laos, Yunnan and Burma.

Classical Empires

By the 10th century, the Tai were gradually becoming a part of the fabric of Southeast Asia, although not yet considered a distinct entity in their own right. They seem to have interacted with several powerful kingdoms of the time, including China, the Khmer Angkor Empire, the northern Vietnamese kingdom of Nam Viet and the Vietnamese kingdom of Champa. The Tai peoples were probably involved in the politics and culture of these empires. It is even possible that Tai groups served in their armies or were war prisoners or slaves.

By the 11th century, the Tai peoples had entered what is now Thailand. The land was already inhabited by Mon- and Khmer-speaking peoples who had arrived centuries earlier. During the 11th and 12th centuries, the Tai peoples were influenced by the great Classical Empires of the time: India; the Mon Empire of Pagan (in present-day Myanmar, or Burma); and the Khmer Angkor Empire (in present-day Cambodia). The Indian civilisation was beginning to have a significant impact on the world, chiefly through the spread of Hinduism, the rise of Indian architecture and the construction of great Indian monuments. It was also the age of the Indian-influenced complexes of Angkor and the Buddhist temples and shrines of Pagan, as well as of the Khmer kings Suryavarman I and II and Jayavarman VII. These influences—of Indianisation, Hinduism, Buddhism and Mon and Khmer cultures—would be evident on the development of the Tai peoples, languages and culture for centuries to come.

Dvaravati: A Buddhist Civilisation

The foundations for Buddhism in central Southeast Asia were laid between the 6th and 9th centuries, when a Theravada Buddhist culture linked to the Mon group was developing in central and northeastern Thailand. Theravadins believe that enlightenment can be obtained only by one living the life of a monk (and not by a layman). Unlike Mahayana Buddhists, who worship numerous buddhas and bodhisattvas, Theravadins worship only the Buddha Gautama, the founder of the religion. The Mon Buddhist kingdoms that rose in what are now parts of Laos and the Central Plain of Thailand were collectively called Dvaravati. In Nakhon Pathom and Suphanburi, coins inscribed with the phrase "Lord of Dvaravati" have been uncovered. Other archaeological sites in northeastern Thailand contain Dvaravati relics of Mon writings, the remains of Buddhist architecture and artifacts such as small Buddhist votive tablets.

Historians believe that the Tai peoples had some contact with the Dvaravati civilisation. Dvaravati inscriptions dating back to the 11th century mention the Tai peoples. The beginnings of interaction among geographically separate parts of Southeast Asia can be traced back to Dvaravati times. There may have been trade, communication and other forms of contact among the Gulf of Thailand, the Upper Mekong (Chiang Mai and Lamphun), the middle Mekong (Khorat Plateau), and perhaps even Vietnam, Yunnan in China and Champa in Burma.

The Angkor Empire

By the end of the 9th century, the Khmer kingdom of Angkor (established by Jayavarman II in the early 9th century) had grown powerful and organised enough to overtake Dvaravati supremacy in central Southeast Asia. The formidable political control exercised by the Angkor Empire extended not only over the centre of the Khmer Province, where the majority of the population was Khmer, but also to outer border provinces likely populated by non-Khmer peoples—including areas to the north and northeast of modern Bangkok, the lower Central Plain and the upper Pink River in the Lamphun-Chiang Mai region.

During the 11th and 12th centuries, the kingdom of Angkor continued to thrive and expand. Theravada Buddhism, the religion of the Khmer Empire, became an established element in Southeast Asian society. Large Buddhist monasteries were built throughout Khmer territory. The culture and practices of the Theravada form of Buddhism of the Mon and Ceylonese (Sri Lankan) cultures predominated, although there were also traces of the Mahayana Buddhist experience, specifically in the influence of the Sanskrit language as opposed to the Pali language of the Theravada.

The Tai peoples were the predominant non-Khmer groups in the areas of central Thailand that formed the geographical periphery of the Khmer Empire. Tai groups were probably assimilated into the Khmer population. Historical records show that they maintained their cultural distinctiveness, although their animist religion partially gave way to Buddhism. Tai historical documents note that the period of the Angkor Empire was one of great internal strife. During the 11th and 12th centuries, territories with a strong Tai presence, such as Lopburi (in what is now north-central Thailand), resisted Khmer control.

LOPBURI, THE RELUCTANT VASSAL

Lopburi had been a Dvaravati captital. Former Buddhist monks from Lopburi had founded the state of Haripunjaya at Lamphun in the 7th century. The king of Lopburi had sent his daughter Camadevi, along with Mon advisors, to create there what eventually became a dynasty that lasted until the middle of the 11th century.

In the early 11th century, Lopburi was seized by a Cambodian prince and made part of the Khmer kingdom of Angkor. However, Lopburi wanted liberation and sought acknowledgement from China in 1001 and 1155 as an independent state. Lopburi's large Tai population and its roots in the Dvaravati Empire did not assimilate well with the Khmer civilisation, and in Khmer writings Lopburi was considered a province of Angkor that had a "Syamese" (Siamese) identity.

Other territories controlled by Tai lords also became prominent. Historical records tell of Prince Phrom, son of the ruler of Chiang Saen (northern Thailand today, bordering the Mekong). During the 10th century, Chiang Saen was a small principality under Khmer control. In the early 11th century, however, Prince Phrom led a revolt against the Khmer and succeeded. He had good ties with local rulers along the western perimeter of the Chao Phraya River, including integral alliances in the towns of Suphanburi and Phetburi. These chiefs and princes later established Tai lands in Nakhon Si Thammarat on the Malay Peninsula and other towns in the Central Plain, such as Chainat, Phitsanulok and Nakhon Sawan.

By the 12th century, the Tai peoples were continuing in their traditional rice-farming activities and establishing urban centres. Historical documents note that new Tai "states" were emerging throughout northern Southeast Asia. Wars and battles were taking place among the Angkor Empire, the Pagan Empire and Vietnam. Settled in the rural fringes of the Angkor and Pagan Empires and in upper Laos, the Tai peoples, united by their lords, were becoming a formidable threat to the powerful kingdoms of the time. Despite intermarriages between the Tai and the Khmer ruling families, the Tai people kept their distinct cultural and ethnic identity, retaining their own languages and units of social organisation.

THE SUKHOTHAI ERA (1238–1378)

The empires of Angkor and Pagan were very powerful at the beginning of the 13th century. However, as the century progressed, this power began to wane. The Tai peoples started to move from the upland valleys and founded new states on the Central Plain—from Assam in the north to central Laos in the east and as far south as Nakhon Si Thammarat, on the Malay Peninsula. There was overwhelming support and provision for the monastic institutions of Theravada Buddhism at this time.

As the supremacy of the Khmer and Pagan Empires lessened, a growing number of smaller states emerged, sharing power more equally. Stone inscriptions and Tai historical records suggest that the Tai peoples were becoming a significant political entity during this period.

Sukhothai and the South

Sukhothai (in north-central Thailand) was one of the earliest and most important settlements in mainland Southeast Asia. Tai peoples settled successfully throughout the Central Plain (or Chao Phraya River basin) during the 13th century because they had already been living there in Dvaravati and Lopburi, and they had an understanding of the social and political aspects of the Angkor Empire. Through the influence of Khmer politics and culture, especially Theravada Buddhism, the Tai who had settled in the Central Plain developed differently from other Tai groups to the north or south. More sophisticated, they quickly supplemented their traditional animistic beliefs with Indian-influenced Theravada Buddhist beliefs. These Tai were called "Siamese", from a modification of the "Syam" noted in Khmer and Pagan writings.

The Tai lords expanded their *müang* by direct conquest as well as through marriage between the Tai elite class and the royal families of other empires. Tai princes and chiefs in the Central Plain were often given official titles—and a wife from the ruling class at Angkor—in return for their allegiance and loyalty to the empire. Pha Muang was one example. He became the king of Sukhothai after staging a revolt against Khmer rule there. Later, his son Ban Muang succeeded him. Sukhothai remained a small local power until the death of Ban Muang. Ramkhamhaeng (Rama the Bold) became the third ruler of Sukhothai in 1279.

The kingdom that Ramkhamhaeng inherited most likely included the city of Sukhothai and the nearby towns of Sawankhalok, Uttaradit, Kamphaengphet and Tak. The new king was ambitious, committed and determined, but also good to his subjects, who enjoyed a just and prosperous society and a comfortable lifestyle. The king was often referred to as "Lord Father".

Sukhothai is renowned for its art and culture. Sculptures of Buddhist images were created, in standing and 'walking' poses. Potters from China were brought to Sukhothai to demonstrate and teach their techniques, creating works in Celadon and Sangkhalok pottery. The court preserved ties with Ceylon (the origins of Theravada Buddhism) and at the same time acknowledged the influence of Hinduism (encompassing Brahmanism). Sculptures of Vishnu and Siva, two of the main Hindu deities, were commissioned. Above all, although there were non-Tai communities of Mon and Khmer with their own ethos, traditions and customs, the kingdom was quintessentially Tai in that Ramkhamhaeng successfully blended politics and Buddhism. The government actively and generously supported Buddhist activities, building many monasteries. The official language was Siamese Tai.

Ramkhamhaeng's writings describe the development of his kingdom and were addressed to various leaders in Phitsanulok, Lom Sak and Viang Chan (later Vientiane) to the east; Nakhon Sawan, Chainat, Suphanburi, Ratburi, Phetburi and Nakhon Si Thammarat to the south; Pegu and Martaban to the west; and Phrae, Nan and Luang Prabang to the north. Ramkhamhaeng probably did not directly control all these towns and cities but had the support of local rulers. Interpersonal allegiances were in great part the prototype of political relationships and expansions in East and Southeast Asia.

On his death in 1298, Ramkhamhaeng's son Lo Thai became king, and the empire Ramkhamhaeng had constructed quickly crumbled. Many of its territories broke away, aiding the rise of the Ayutthaya Kingdom. By 1320, Sukhothai was no longer the significant power it had been under King Ramkhamhaeng.

The Kingdom of Lan Na

Sukhothai was not the only Tai kingdom to rise to power in mainland Southeast Asia in the 13th century. The kingdom of Lan Na was founded in 1259 by Mangrai, the son of the Lao ruler of Chiang Saen. Mangrai's mother had been the daughter of the Tai lord of Chiang Hung, in Yunnan. Bordering this kingdom were Vietnam to the east, Nan Chao (now in Yunnan) to the north, Haripunjaya (now Lamphun) to the south and the Shan regions to the west.

King Mangrai expanded his control over neighbouring states and founded the city of Chiang Rai in 1262, moving his capital there. In 1274 he patiently devised a long-term plan to capture the principality of Haripunjaya and was rewarded in 1281 in securing the north. Mangrai developed the region's administration and defence, building cities, monasteries and the army. In 1289 he conquered Pegu, the capital of the Mon region of lower Burma. Mangrai married the daughter of Suddhasoma, the king of Pegu. In 1292 Mangrai moved his royal residence to Chiang Mai, making it the new capital of his kingdom. Construction of the city of Chiang Mai began in 1296 due to perceived threats from the Mongols against his kingdom. The ruling class of Mangrai's kingdom was Tai, but there were strong communities of Mon, Lawa, and other hill peoples, as well as a non-ruling Tai contingent.

Mangrai was a patron of Mon culture and a supporter of Theravada Buddhism. During his reign, he built a powerful kingdom that resisted the threat of Mongol invasion and had far-reaching effects on other Tai peoples, especially in the spread of Theravada Buddhism to the Shan and Khoen in Burma, the Tai Lü in Yunnan and the Kao and Lao in Laos and China. "The Judgements of King Mangrai", laws instituted during his reign, are still considered practical and compassionate today.

Mangrai died in 1317, reputedly struck by lightning. Although few, if any, of the later rulers in his dynasty proved as competent and powerful as Mangrai, the kingdom of Lan Na remained an influential and independent political power until it was conquered by Burma in the 16th century.

Tai diplomacy sometimes managed to avert war. Mangrai of Lan Na originally planned to take the kingdom of Phayao (to the southeast) by force, but instead he struck up a friendship of mutual benefit with the ruler of Phayao, Ngam Muang. Ngam peacefully relinquished a frontier district to Mangrai. Ngam in turn had become acquainted with King Ramkhamhaeng of Sukhothai during their religious studies in Lopburi. When there was a personal disagreement between Ramkhamhaeng and Ngam Muang years later, Mangrai mediated, resolving the dispute peacefully. The three rulers promised everlasting friendship to one another, realising they had joint, albeit separate, interests and purposes. Their common Tai descent and identity was a binding element in their friendship.

THE AYUTTHAYA PERIOD (1351–1767)

The city of Ayutthaya was established in 1351. The Royal Chronicles of Ayutthaya named U Thong (Ramathibodi I) as founder and first king of Ayutthaya. The reign of Ramathibodi I (r. 1351–1369) saw the fortification of the eastern frontiers against the Khmer Angkor Empire. At this time, Ayutthaya was the centre of the Lopburi region, independent of Sukhothai and of Angkor. Its strategic location on the rich plain of the Chao Phraya River basin contributed to its increasing success and importance as a trading centre. Ayutthaya, increasingly synonymous with "Siam", would dominate politics and culture in mainland Southeast Asia for the next 400 years. Its culture was a fusion of Mahayana and Theravada Buddhism, Khmer Brahmanism and Indian arts and sciences. The population comprised Mon, Tai and Khmer peoples. On the western side of the Chao Phraya River was Suphanburi, a primarily Tai state and a stronghold of Theravada Buddhism.

Ramathibodi I is credited with laying the foundations for a Siamese legal system. He introduced several civic and state laws. His death in 1369 brought a succession of Siamese kings who continued to develop and expand Ayutthaya. Under King Borommaracha II (r. 1424–1448), Ayutthaya attacked and defeated Angkor in 1431, bringing back to the city many Khmer prisoners, including former officials of the Khmer royal court. Khmer-Hindu influence led to the adoption in Ayutthaya of Hindu practices such as the devaraja, the idea of the ruler as divine god-king. This greatly strengthened the image and power of Ayutthayan kings.

In 1438, Ayutthaya conquered the kingdom of Sukhothai, replacing it as the foremost kingdom in the region. In the latter part of the 15th century, the main threats to Ayutthaya came from other parts of the Tai world—the kingdoms of Lan Na to the north and Lan Sang (with its capital at Luang Prabang and occupying what is now northwestern Laos and northeastern Thailand).

King Borommatrailokanat, or Trailok, the son and successor of Borommaracha II, ruled Ayutthaya from 1448 to 1488. During his reign, Tai society developed a strict hierarchical order. His laws ascribed every individual a place and position in society. Each person was assigned units called *sakdi na* ("field power"), designating his or her social rank. For example, slaves received a *sakdi na* of five; petty officials 50–400; state ministers 10,000; and the king's heir at least 100,000.

Lan Na and Conflict with Neighbouring Powers

The kingdom of Lan Na faced internal and external struggles throughout the 14th and 15th centuries. The 30-year period from 1320 to 1350 saw King Mangrai's successors undergo a series of abdications. From 1367 to 1385, Lan Na flourished once again, under the rule of King Ku Na. Well-educated in the Indic arts and sciences, Ku Na invited the Venerable Sumana—a Sukhothai monk—to set up a Sinhalese (from Ceylon) order in Lamphun, and the king built a monastery for him. This Buddhist sect became a significant cultural and religious influence in Lan Na, contributing much of the written text from this time period. It also provided the northern Tai a strong regional sense of identity.

In 1404 and 1405, the Chinese governor of Yunnan sent troops to Chiang Saen. Lan Na, ruled at this time by the grandson of Ku Na, Sam Fang Kaen, managed to fend off the attacks. The rest of Sam Fang Kaen's reign was peaceful for the most part, and he continued to fortify his kingdom by sending his sons to govern the major principalities.

In 1441, Sam Fang Kaen's sixth son overthrew him to become King Tilokaracha (r. 1442–1487). King Tilok warded off attacking Ayutthayan forces in Lamphun, but he and Ayutthaya's King Trailok repeatedly failed to reach a truce. Each side sent spies to undermine the other. By the time of Tilok's death in 1487 and Trailok's a year later, struggles between Lan Na and Ayutthaya seemed to have reached a stalemate.

Although Lan Na remained independent until Burmese conquest in the 16th century, the kingdom was becoming increasingly vulnerable to aggression, especially from Ayutthaya and from the Shan peoples who had started to move into the Chiang Saen region.

The Arrival of the Portuguese

Ayutthaya continued to gain momentum as a power following the death of King Trailok and throughout the reigns of his sons Intharacha (r. 1488–91) and Ramathibodi II (r. 1491–1529). The kingdom had an imposing authority over the Malay Peninsula and the coast of the Bay of Bengal, and it enjoyed an overall state of prosperity through trade that continued to increase significantly during the 15th and 16th centuries. Noteworthy religious monuments were constructed during the early part of the 16th century, including the largest standing metal image of Buddha (16 m high) encased in gold.

In 1511, following their takeover of Malacca in the Malay Peninsula, the Portuguese sent their first mission to Ayutthaya. They were well received, and after several subsequent missions, a peace pact between Ayutthaya and Portugal was signed. The Portuguese were given permission for residence and religious freedom in Ayutthaya and numerous good commercial opportunities. In return, the Portuguese supplied firearms to Ayutthaya (and also to its chief adversaries). An increase in communication, travel and trade for Ayutthaya helped spread the Siamese culture beyond the capital to many parts of mainland Southeast Asia, as far south as the Malay Peninsula.

The Burmese Threat

Lan Na launched attacks on Ayutthaya in 1507, 1508 and 1515. Through to the mid-16th century, Ayutthayan politics were dominated by court intrigue and its resulting instability. In the mid-16th century, both the Burmese and the Khmer king of Lawaek along the eastern border attacked Ayutthaya. Ayutthaya fortified the capital walls, improved military might and mobilised its military force to Lawaek from 1555 to secure its eastern borders. However, through various conquests in the Shan states, Burma secured a strategic position on the northern borders of the Tai kingdoms.

In 1558, Burma took Lan Na as a vassal, using it to become a commanding presence on the western frontier. It was from here that the Burmese repelled Ayutthaya and Lan Sang. Although Lan Na would eventually rejoin the Siamese kingdom in the 19th century, King Mangrai's dynasty was brought to a close. The Burmese, under King Bayinnaung (r. 1551–1581) attacked and captured several northern cities, overrunning Ayutthaya in 1569. The Tai world was in serious disarray; several Tai groups had in fact joined forces with the Burmese against Ayutthaya.

After Burmese conquest in 1569, Ayutthaya was looted. Both nobility and commoners were taken to Burma as prisoners. The Khmer Cambodians invaded the kingdom six times in the next 20 years, and prisoners were taken from the more affluent Ayutthayan provinces, including the region from Chanthaburi to Phetburi. Recognising the vulnerability of their vassal to other invaders, the Burmese re-fortified the walls of Ayutthaya.

The Restoration of Ayutthaya

The reign of King Naresuan (r. 1590–1605) in Ayutthaya restored the kingdom to independence after decades of disgrace. Naresuan was the driving force behind significant social and political changes in Ayutthaya. In 1584, he declared Ayutthaya no longer a Burmese vassal and successfully warded off Burmese and Cambodian attacks to secure Ayutthaya's independence. In the Battle of Nong Sarai (some 20 km northwest of Suphanburi) in 1593, Naresuan fought a duel on elephant-back with the heir to the Burmese throne and killed him. The ensuing succession dispute allowed Naresuan to expand Ayutthaya into the peninsular regions of Burma.

Ayutthaya continued to be vigilant in its defences, practising a strategy of dividing its adversaries and conquering. By this time it was an important commercial centre, and prosperous trade continued to make it stronger and more powerful. The kingdom imported weapons from Japan and Portugal and had a powerful navy in the 16th and early-17th centuries. King Naresuan had a keen understanding of international politics, playing China against possible invasions of Ayutthaya by the Japanese, while keeping a close eye on possible aggression from Burma and Cambodia; Thai records refer to him as "Naresuan the Great". When he died in 1605, his brother Ekathotsarot (r. 1605–1611) inherited a strong and vital kingdom. Ekathotsarot received the first Dutch ships at his ports and sent the first Siamese diplomatic mission to the Netherlands and to Portuguese Goa.

Foreign Relations and the Phaulkon Affair

Between 1611 and 1656, the Ayutthayan palace was rocked by power upheavals, some of them violent. To place Ayutthaya increasingly in the international trade and political arena, the Ayutthayan kings had started appointing foreign experts to manage their foreign commerce. English East India Company ships arrived at Ayutthaya in 1612 and established factories in Ayutthaya and Patani, a Muslim state in what is now southern Thailand. There was a large and dense contingent of foreigners in Ayutthaya, including the Dutch and Chinese. In 1656, Prince Narai (r. 1656–1688) became king, allegedly through the support of Japanese, Thais, Patani Malays and Persians. During his reign, many missions were sent to Persia, India and China, and, from 1662, French Jesuit missionaries were allowed into Ayutthaya. They were permitted to advocate Christianity and operate a seminary. In exchange, they provided technical assistance to Ayutthaya.

In 1678, Greek adventurer Constantine Phaulkon arrived in Ayutthaya with the English East India Company. A gifted interpreter, he gained the favour of King Narai and quickly rose to the highest position in the civil service, that of the Mahattani, greatly influencing Narai's foreign policy. Narai granted the French numerous trade privileges, including permission to station French troops in the town of Singora (Songkhla) in 1685. In collaboration with French Roman Catholic Jesuit missionaries, Phaulkon wanted to convert King Narai to Christianity and increase French power in Ayutthaya, but he was also skilful at pitting different players against one other for his own personal gain.

Phaulkon further ingratiated himself with King Narai by thwarting a Makasarese plot against the throne in 1686. (The Makasarese originated in Celebes in Indonesia. A group of these Muslim traders, ousted by the Dutch, had settled in Siam.) That year, Siam sent a mission to France. In response the French made more demands on King Narai in 1687. The French sent troops to Bangkok and the port of Mergui on the Tenasserim coast to pressure the king into accepting these demands.

Relations between Siam and the English East India Company, meanwhile, had grown so strained over disputed trading interests in southern India that a conflict erupted in Mergui in 1687. In the Mergui Massacre, as it came to be called, 60 Englishmen from the English East India Company were killed by Siamese officials. King Narai declared war on the East India Company and decided to install a French governor and French troops in Mergui.

Yet Siamese-French relations were deteriorating too. In Ayutthaya, the Siamese people were becoming increasingly disgruntled over their king's foreign connections. They did not like that Phaulkon, a Greek Christian, was a powerful minister and key player in the government. They were unhappy that although Phaulkon was a close friend of King Narai, he was more loyal to foreign and Christian elements than to the king and Siam. When Narai fell ill before dying in 1688, anti-French elements led by Phetracha, who was like a foster brother to Narai, executed Phaulkon.

Phetracha seized the throne in a coup in 1688. His foreign policy sought to reinforce traditional values by drastically curbing the presence and activities of European powers in Siam. He had French troops removed and Christians persecuted.

OTHER TAI KINGDOMS

To the north of Ayutthaya, the Tai kingdoms of Lan Sang and Lan Na still existed. Lan Na had become a vassal of Burma in the 16th century, but Lan Sang was enjoying a time of prosperity. Towards the end of the 16th century, Lan Na began to struggle against Burmese control, taking advantage of regular attacks on Pegu by Siam's King Naresuan during the 1590s. At the request of Lan Sang, Naresuan offered to place Lan Na under Siamese protection and assigned a Lao noble as a Siamese commissioner there. Despite this, conflicts with Burma continued, and this was a difficult time for the Tai kingdoms.

On his death in 1703, Phetracha was succeeded by Suriyentharathibodi, or King Sua (The Tiger King), a bad-tempered, bloodthirsty tyrant. The 18th century brought limited improvements within Siam. Trade with China prospered and Buddhism was strengthened, but the Siamese kings did little to fortify the kingdom against the Burmese threat that King Naresuan had held at bay. In 1767, the Burmese attacked Ayutthaya again and sacked the city, taking King Borommaracha (r. 1758–1767) and thousands of Siamese people captive and destroying most of the city's works of art and historical records. The kingdom of Ayutthaya collapsed.

THE THON BURI PERIOD (1767–1772)

When Ayutthaya fell to the Burmese in 1767, a Chinese-Siamese man named Sin was serving as governor of the Tak province. Phraya Tak (Sin), or Taksin, was an astute and forceful military leader who gathered fresh troops from the southeastern reaches of the Siamese kingdom and pushed back Burmese forces to take political power. He moved the new capital to Thon Buri in 1767. Located strategically on the Chao Phraya River and on the opposite bank to Bangkok, Thon Buri was considered less accessible to Burmese forces than Bangkok. Under Taksin's rule, Siam recovered all of the conquered Ayutthayan territories from Burma. He successfully claimed the kingdom of Lan Na, driving the Burmese from what is now Chiang Mai. He also extended his territory into Laos and Cambodia. Taksin encouraged strong support for Chinese trade, and many Chinese business- and tradespeople settled permanently in Siam, building its economy.

Taksin was a successful conquerer. He gave the Siamese military a sound structural framework and his relations with the Chinese allowed the Siamese kingdom to prosper. His arbitrary laws, however, and his pretension at having nearly attained buddha status left many of his subjects and Buddhist monks dissatisfied. An uprising in Cambodia in 1781 resulted in the death of its king and subsequent widespread chaos. Taksin wanted to place a pro-Siamese king on the throne and sent 20,000 troops to get the job done. His plan backfired, however, and rebel forces turned on Taksin and the capital city, calling for Taksin's removal from power and for the accession of his chief general in Cambodia, Chao Phraya Chakri. Taksin was executed and buried, but rumour has it that he was instead secreted to a mountain retreat where he lived until 1825.

THE RATTANOKOSIN ERA (1782–PRESENT)

THE EARLY CHAKRI DYNASTY

Rama I (r. 1782–1809)

Chao Phraya Chakri, or Phra Phutthayotfa Chulalok, is better known today as Rama I—the first king of the Chakri Dynasty. During his reign, the capital was moved from Thon Buri back to Bangkok.

Tension between Burma and Siam continued, and in 1785 Burma launched a substantial attack against Siam. Although Burma was defeated, subsequent smaller assaults were also attempted. It was the British who in the 1820s were finally able to contain Burmese forces and stop the attacks.

Rama I was heralded for the significant architectural and cultural advances made during his reign. He was responsible for the building of the Grand Palace, commissioning the mural paintings of the *Ramakien* (the Thai translation of the Indian *Ramayana* epic) story there and establishing a placement in Bangkok for the Emerald Buddha, a famous statue that had previously been housed in Chiang Rai and Chiang Mai. A skilled poet and benefactor of the arts, Rama I renewed the importance of Buddhism, which had been neglected by Taksin. He supported the education of monks and the building of temples, as well as the ratification of ecclesiastical laws and guidelines. He also codified Siamese law and strengthened the administration and the military. Rama I died in September 1809 and was succeeded by his eldest son, Prince Itsarasunthon.

Rama II (r. 1809–1824)

Prince Itsarasunthon, or Phra Phutthaloetla Naphalai, had been an active participant in government during his father's reign, and he had significant skill and knowledge of the Siamese kingdom. Himself a distinguished poet, Rama II supported the development of culture and the arts.

SIAM IN THE EARLY 19TH CENTURY

Siam expanded geographically during the reigns of both Rama I and Rama II. Relations with Burma on the western frontier were relatively quiet, but there was increasing concern and unrest on the eastern side of the kingdom, between Siam and Vietnam. Western powers, shut out of Siam since the Phaulkon Affair, stood poised on Siam's doorstep, with a Dutch presence in Batavia (Jakarta); Portuguese traders and French Roman Catholic missionaries active in other parts of Southeast Asia; and the British in Penang. When Singapore became a free port under the control of the English East India Company in 1819, trade between Siam and the Malay Peninsula were optimal for development and growth.

Rama III (r. 1824–1851)

Prince Chetsadabodin, or Phra Nangklao, was made king in 1824 because he was much older and more experienced than his younger half-brother Mongkut, although the latter had a stronger claim to the throne. As king, Rama III retained most of his father's ministers and kept military and foreign affairs at the top of Siam's agenda. Britain was in conflict with Burma over Burmese attacks on India, and Rama III was concerned that Britain might be planning to attack Siam too. He had blacksmiths construct an iron chain stretching across the Chao Phraya River mouth to protect the country. During the reign of Rama III, Siam reached its largest geographical extent. Rama III consolidated control over land in the Malay Peninsula and launched attacks on Viang Chan (Vientiane) to the northeast. Many Lao prisoners were brought to Siam.

Relations between Siam and the West, which had long been stagnant, were officially renewed by Rama III. In 1826, the Burney Treaty formally established trade between Siam and Britain. Rama III signed this agreement in part out of fear that Britain would declare war on Siam as it had done on Burma in 1824. The Burney Treaty marked a crossroads of sorts for Siam; it was the first authorised agreement officially establishing a framework and guidelines for diplomatic and trade relations between Siam and the West.

In 1827, Lao troops attacked Siam, but Siamese forces were quickly deployed and, several months later, Siam victoriously occupied Vientiane. Most of the city was destroyed, leaving only the Buddhist temples relatively unscathed. Most of the people from Vientiane were relocated to the provinces of Lopburi, Saraburi, Suphanburi and Nakhon Chaisi in Siam.

In the southern Malay Peninsula, Siam responded to unrest by extending the governing authority of the Malay rajas (local rulers) there. This gradually reduced some of Siam's influence in that region, creating more of a balance between Siamese and local oversight. Conflicts and battles with Cambodia and Vietnam continued and escalated.

Although Rama III earned some notoriety as a non-supporter of secular literature and the arts—especially with his exile of great Thai poet Sunthorn Phu—Siam made some significant cultural strides during his reign. In his restoration of Wat Phrachetuphon (Wat Po) in Bangkok, he commissioned engravings and murals to adorn the walls. He was also a generous patron of writings on science, religion, the military, politics and traditional medicine. His reign has been labelled conservative and intransigent, but in fact he did much to preserve traditional culture and values. Rama III died in 1851, fully expecting that Prince Mongkut would succeed him as king.

Rama IV (Mongkut) (r. 1851–1868)

Prince Mongkut was only 20 and a young Buddhist monk when his father died and his half-brother Chetsadabodin became king. Mongkut was a scholar proficient in the Pali language, the ancient language of Buddhist sacred writings. Convinced that many non-essential practices had sprung up around core Theravada teachings, Mongkut and a group of fellow monks were inspired to follow the teachings of early Buddhism as reflected in the

Mon discipline of the Thammayutika. Mongkut became abbot of the Wat Bowonniwet, establishing a separate order of Siamese monks, the Thammayut sect, who practised a reformed Theravada Buddhism. In time, Mongkut's *wat* (monastery) became an important centre for Western science, languages and learning.

THE CALL OF THE WEST

Rama IV, and to a lesser extent Rama III before him, did not view the West with the distrust and hatred that had existed during the time of Taksin. Mongkut was convinced that cooperation with the Europeans would preserve the freedom and independence of Siam. By the 1820s, European knowledge and technical skills were beginning to influence and inspire the Siamese elite. Western-style square-rigged sailing boats were gradually being substituted for the traditional Chinese ships in commerce. Prince Wongsathirat (Mongkut's half-brother) studied Western medicine, and Prince Chudamani (Mongkut's brother) managed military troops according to European methods and practices.

During the reign of Rama IV, friendly relations with the West continued with the signing of the Bowring Treaty in 1855. This provided for the opening of a British consulate in Bangkok to take care of matters concerning citizens of Great Britain who resided in Siam. In part, Siam also hoped the treaty would offer some defence against designs on the kingdom by other world powers. In particular, Mongkut wanted to balance French and English interests in the Southeast Asian region. When King Duong from Cambodia died in 1860, the French instituted colonial rule in southern Vietnam, and in 1863, Vietnam became a protectorate of France.

Rama IV allowed foreign advisors and workers in his court. He engaged an English tutor, Anna Leonowens, for his children. Expatriates, including missionaries, began to set up long-term residences in Bangkok. The capital had by now grown from a small village during the time of Taksin to a city of approximately 400,000, many of whom were Chinese immigrants. Missionaries set up schools, medical facilities and printing presses. Mongkut published a government gazette in which the laws of the kingdom were printed so that they would be accessible to the public. To better understand and care for his subjects, the king travelled extensively throughout his kingdom. Unlike the kings before him, subjects were permitted to look directly at Mongkut.

King Rama V (Chulalongkorn) (r. 1868–1910)

Unexpectedly, both Mongkut and his young heir Prince Chulalongkorn contracted malaria during a visit to the Malay Peninsula, and Mongkut died in October 1868. Prince Chulalongkorn was then just 15 years old, and Chao Phraya Si Suriyawong (Mongkut's effective prime minister) became his regent. In 1873, Chulalongkorn was officially crowned king of Siam (Rama V).

Rama V faced strong Western political pressure and was forced to deal diplomatically with these demands. In 1893 he surrendered Siam's Lao territories east of the Mekong River to France, at which time the French also took the Lao territories west of the Mekong River and in northwestern Cambodia. During the reign of Rama V, the British took over from Siam the rights of four Malay states.

Other changes were also taking place in Siamese government and society. Ministries with specific responsibilities were organised, and a centralised system of government administering the provinces was created. Tax laws were standardised and slavery and labour-service requirements eradicated. Railway and telegraph systems were established. A modern education system was introduced. Rama V also supported the reorganisation of the Buddhist monkhood. The national currency, the Thai baht, was introduced in 1897.

The reign of Rama V is widely considered one of the most successful periods of Siamese history. Chulalongkorn was responsible for many far-reaching reforms and is credited with building a modern Thailand.

THE HISTORY OF THAI CURRENCY

Most Southeast Asian currency can be traced back to the Funan kingdom that covered parts of what are now Vietnam, Thailand and Cambodia between the 1st and 6th century AD. The coins were modelled after Hindu silver coins and featured an image of the sun and a representation of the Hindu god Vishnu. Coins from the later Dvaravati and Srivijaya (Sumatra and the Malay Peninsula) kingdoms introduced and depicted more varied motifs.

Early Siamese coins borrowed heavily from Funan, Dvaravati and Srivijaya designs. Silver (and sometimes brass or even tin) money was used in the Lan Chang kingdom of Laos and northeastern Siam. The kingdom of Lan Na used a brass and silver currency.

A "flower" coin of higher-quality silver was also made, featuring decorations of flowers on one side and indentations on the other. Bracelet-shaped money—too small for the wrist but thought to be derived from larger originals worn like bracelets for safekeeping— was probably made by private merchants.

In Sukhothai and Ayutthaya, bullet coins were used—silver currency moulded into a circular "cowry shell" shape similar to that of a signet ring. Each coin had a different weight, and this determined their value. During the Thon Buri era and the reign of King Taksin, coins featured the Buddhist Wheel of Law.

Flat two-sided coins began to be used alongside bullet coins during the reign of King Rama III. Rama IV made foreign-issued coins legal tender in Siam. During his reign, the first machine-produced coins were issued, in gold and silver.

Today, the national currency of Thailand is the baht. One baht consists of 100 smaller units called *satang*. Before the baht was introduced in 1897, the Thai monetary system was much more complicated. The largest unit, the *chung*, was subdivided into 20 tambling. The *tambling* was further subdivided into smaller units.

Rama VI (Vajiravudh) (r. 1910–1925)

In 1910, when Chulalongkorn died, his son and successor Vajiravudh was a 17-year-old student in Oxford, England. An avid supporter of the arts, Rama VI wrote a chapter of the *Ramayana* in Thai, studied traditional literature extensively and authored several scholarly articles. He was also responsible for many progressive reforms. A strong proponent of education, he made primary education compulsory. He also elevated the

Civil Service Institution (established in 1899 by Chulalongkorn to train civil servants for government work) and renamed it Chulalongkorn University, in memory of his father.

Nationalism was another of Vajiravudh's key interests. To fully integrate the Chinese who had settled in Siam, the kingdom required that all citizens understand the principles and ethics of being Siamese, including being able to read, write and understand Standard Thai. Vajiravudh introduced a new Thai flag; the previous flag had featured a white elephant, traditionally a Thai symbol of good fortune, on a red background. The new flag contained horizontal stripes of red, white, blue, white and red. Vajiravudh also created two new national holidays: Chulalongkorn Day (October 23), in honour of his father; and Chakri Day (April 6), in honour of the Chakri Dynasty, of which he was the sixth king. He popularised the expression "Thai Nation", combining the notions of nation, religion and monarch.

As Siam continued to modernise under the sovereignty of Rama VI, a law in 1913 made it mandatory for all Thais to have a surname, and citizens were urged to adopt more modern rather than traditional attire. Reiterating the need for all Siamese to be loyal to their country, Vajiravudh strengthened the armed forces. Siam joined World War I (1914–1918) on the side of the Allies in 1917, and thereafter Vajiravudh worked diligently to convince the Western powers to relinquish their extraterritorial rights in Siam.

Although Siam made great strides during his reign, some groups were critical of Vajiravudh's perceived loyalty to aspects of westernisation and of his extravagant ways. He survived an abortive plot by military officials against the throne in 1912. In 1925, his brother Prajadhipok, the youngest of Mongkut's 32 sons, became king.

Rama VII (Prajadhipok) (r. 1925–1932)

As Rama VII, Prajadhipok inherited the throne at a time when the absolute monarchy was increasingly under scrutiny and challenge from a growing print forum. Newspapers and magazines in English, Thai and Chinese criticised the power, actions and methods of absolute monarchy. At this time, political debate and ideas were also strong among foreign Asian communities in Siam. Some Chinese were involved in anti-Japanese campaigns, others in discussion about communism and Kuomintangism. Siam was also a centre for nationals of Vietnam, Laos, Cambodia and Burma who challenged their home-country politics and colonial governments, using Siam as their base of operations.

Foremost in Siam was the growing dissatisfaction of a group of overseas-educated Thai who challenged the supremacy of the royal family. This group of Thai students, led by Pridi Phanomyong and Luang Phibun Songkhram (Phibunsongkhram), formed a political party called the People's Party in 1932. Its ultimate goal was to remove the monarchy from Siam. On 24 June 1932, while Rama VII was away from Bangkok, the People's Party led a coup against the government, forcing the king to accept a constitution. In 1934, Prajadhipok left Siam and abdicated the following year. Prince Ananda Mahidol became King Rama VIII (r. 1935–1946), but because he was only a boy of 10 at the time, a regency council was appointed until he came of age.

LUANG PHIBUN SONGKHRAM (1938–1944) AND POST-WAR GOVERNMENTS

Luang Phibun Songkhram became the military dictator and prime minister of Siam in December 1938. His cabinet comprised 25 men, more than half of whom had a military background or agenda. His plan was to build a *sang chat* (new nation), and to this end he changed the country's name from Siam to Thailand in 1939. His policies were fiercely nationalistic. In 1940, Thailand occupied and gained control over French territories in western Laos and northwestern Cambodia. World War II, however, changed the political climate throughout all of Southeast Asia.

On 7 December 1941, the Japanese attacked Pearl Harbor, and on 8 December Japanese troops entered Thailand demanding right of passage through the country to attack British-held Singapore. After a brief resistance, Thailand signed a Treaty of Alliance with Japan in 1942, declaring war on Britain and the United States.

Thailand's economy was in tatters by 1944. The Thai people, seeing Phibun as a Japanese sympathiser, had little confidence in him. Resistance groups in the United States, Britain and Thailand joined forces as the Free Thai to conduct raids against the Japanese. They succeeded in infiltrating the government and, in 1944, Phibun was forced to resign.

Khuang Aphaiwong was appointed prime minister (1944–1946). Khuang was a member of the Khmer family that had ruled western Cambodia since the 18th century. When his homeland was taken over by the French in 1907, Khuang had moved to Thailand. He had been part of the group that had abolished the absolute monarchy in 1932.

The Japanese surrendered in 1945. Although Thailand experienced some international criticism for its alliance with Japan during the war, many countries believed that Thailand had been coerced. The United States maintained goodwill towards Thailand and, upon returning to France the territories seized before the war, Thailand was accepted into the United Nations.

Khuang resigned in 1946 and was replaced by Pridi Phanomyong. That year, the new king, Rama VIII (Ananda Mahidol) was killed by a gunshot wound. Falsely accused of the king's murder, Pridi resigned and left the country. The government changed hands several times between 1946 and 1948.

In 1948 the military, led by Phibun, rose to power again. Phibun made Thailand a watchdog against the spread of communism in Southeast Asia. During the Korean War (1950–1953), Thailand's troops were part of the United Nations forces that fought on the side of South Korea, and Thailand was also a charter member of the anti-communist Southeast Asia Treaty Organization in 1954. On the home front, Phibun kept a close watch on the growth of the communist regime in China. In an effort to curb communism within Thailand, Phibun enforced measures against the Chinese residing in Thailand. Chinese businesses were regulated, as was Chinese immigration into Thailand. Other government opponents, such as leaders of the southern Malay provinces suspected of plotting to break free from Thai rule, faced harassment and incarceration.

The United States contributed huge amounts of financial resources to Thailand between 1951 and 1957 in an effort to bolster the country's internal organisation and improve its military and police forces. The Thai military gained significant momentum during this time, and Phibun became closely aligned with the police and the army chief, Sarit Thanarat. The heavy involvement of many government officials in big business earned the distrust of the Thai people. In 1957, following a bloodless military coup, Sarit took over the government and Phibun fled the country.

MILITARY RULE AND THE MONARCHY

Sarit's dictatorship lasted from 1958 to 1963. With strong foreign economic aid, notably from the United States, Thailand's economy prospered during these years, and the infrastructure of the country—irrigation, roads, and schools—improved.

Communism remained a threat in the region, and Thailand worked closely with the United States to curb its spread. In neighbouring Laos, the leftist Pathet Lao (Lao Country) movement led by Prince Souphanouvong was receiving the support of communist Vietnam. To counter this threat, Thailand supported rightist Lao movements and General Phoumi Nosavan (Sarit's cousin) and closed their borders with Laos. There were also conflicts with Cambodia, particularly a dispute over the border where the Preah Vihear temple was located. The dispute was eventually referred to the International Court of Justice at The Hague. In 1962, the International Court awarded the site to Cambodia.

King Bhumibol Adulyadej, or Rama IX (r. 1946–), succeeded his brother Ananda Mahidol in 1946 and was officially crowned in 1950. Encouraged to offer a more visible profile to the Thai people, King Bhumibol and Queen Sirikit travelled a great deal throughout the country. The monarchy recovered a great deal of its former dignity and significance as a representation of Thailand.

Throughout his term in office, Sarit was respected and esteemed by many. However, upon his death, the extent of his corruption became public. Governments of his successors, Thanom Kittikachorn and Praphas Charusathian, were also corrupt. Thailand allied with the United States during the Vietnam War (1954–1975), sending more than 11,000 troops to Vietnam. The United States continued to contribute significant amounts of money to Thailand. Many commentators assert that this investment not only helped develop the country's economy, but it also worsened the corruption that continued in Thailand and added to the widening gap between the rich and poor. Severe economic issues affecting northeastern Thailand, Muslim Malays in the south and the Hmong hill people in northern Thailand resulted in the formation of insurgency groups.

The 1973 Revolution

In the face of growing unrest, Thanom made minor democratic concessions within his military regime. His measures failed, however, and in 1971 he again imposed military rule. This angered many groups, especially students and an expanding Western-educated middle class. Public demonstrations, many of them violent, demanded a constitution. In 1973 Thanom and Praphas were forced to ask the king to intervene. King Bhumibol restored order, but both Thanom and Praphas left Thailand.

The constitutional monarchy began to play a pivotal and direct role in politics. The king appointed Sanya Dharmasakti as provisional prime minister and a constitution was drawn up in 1974. Thailand experienced a short-lived window of democracy, but as the threat of communism began to gain momentum close to home with communist regimes in power in neighbouring Vietnam, Cambodia and Laos by 1975, the Thai government decided that their best protection was a military government. The king supported this decision, and in 1976 the military took power once again, and both the parliament and constitution were dissolved.

Unrest in Thailand continued. Students and other groups who had stood against the military government in 1973 were very dissatisfied with military rule. They joined the Communist Party of Thailand, which emerged by 1977 as a real threat to the military regime. Deciding to explore a more democratic style, the military government handed power to General Kriangsak Chomanand.

1980–2000

The system of government evolved under Kriangsak and, by 1980 when his successor General Prem Tinsulanonda took over, a system was in place whereby the military governed with the help of a parliament and the mediation of the monarchy. The government officially pardoned all who had been insurgents. This helped restore internal stability to some extent, but just beyond Thailand's borders there were problems. Vietnam had occupied Cambodia in 1979, forcing many refugees across the border into Thailand. This strained resources, personnel and infrastructure in Thailand.

Refugees

In 1988, Chatichai Choonhavan of the Chat Thai Party became the first elected prime minister in 12 years, although the military still retained the power to overturn parliamentary decisions. The Chatichai government was charged with widespread corruption, and in 1991, a military junta calling itself the National Peacekeeping Council overthrew the Chatichai government. Anand Punyarachun, a liberal and former diplomat and businessman, was made prime minister. He could not keep his government independent of the military, however, and in April 1992 army chief Suchinda Krapayoon succeeded Anand. Suchinda's appointment met with widespread public demonstrations that criticised his government as anti-democratic. The king intervened again to restore order. Suchinda resigned and Anand returned to lead a caretaker government. Parties backing an anti-military government attained the majority of seats in parliament, and Chuan Leekpai became the new prime minister. Chuan attempted to redress pervasive conservative and totalitarian policies but was unsuccessful in drafting a constitution before his term ended in 1995.

The 1990s saw the Thai economy thrive despite unstable internal politics. Thailand was poised to join South Korea, Taiwan, Singapore and Hong Kong as newly industrialised economies of Southeast and East Asia. Exports, foreign investment and land prices climbed steadily, but the benefits of a strong economy did not always reach the average urban Thai citizen, who faced worsening traffic congestion, environmental pollution and a widening gap between the rich and poor.

Banharn Silpa-archa became the prime minister in 1995. His term, marked by economic difficulties for Thailand, lasted only a year. His successor was Chavalit Yongchaiyudh, whose equally short tenure saw a collapse of the Thai baht. The country joined many others hit by the Asian currency crisis that began in 1997 when Western investors lost confidence in East Asia and started to withdraw their investments from the region.

During Chavalit's term, a democratic constitution was drafted that included a reduction in senatorial powers, minimum qualifications for government representatives and safeguards to halt corruption. Chavalit resigned in 1997 because of the financial crisis, and Chuan Leekpai again became prime minister, serving his second term from 1997 to 2001. He collaborated closely with the IMF (International Monetary Fund), the result of which was an agreement that steadied the Thai baht at 40:1 against the US dollar by April 1998. The constitution was not ratified during Chuan's second term, in large part due to the political difficulties and corruption that faced his administration.

2000–present

The national elections of January 2001 brought Thaksin Shinawatra and his Thai Rak Thai Party to power. One of Thailand's richest men, Thaksin had been a successful businessman in the fields of computer technology and telecommunications prior to entering politics. His tenure was fraught with issues, both internal and external. In 2003, Thailand embarked on a nationwide effort to rid the country of methamphetamines. The tough tactics of Thai authorities, especially the dealing of the death penalty to large numbers of traffickers, were strongly criticised by human rights activists. That same year, the Southeast Asian region was hit by Severe Acute Respiratory Syndrome (SARS). Thailand had 9 probable cases, with two resulting deaths. Thailand was vigilant in instituting and implementing policies, guidelines and strategies for infection control and public information, and worked closely with international agencies to monitor and contain SARS.

Between 2004 and 2006, Thailand experienced three outbreaks of bird flu totalling 25 cases and 17 resulting deaths. Poultry was culled and the Ministry of Health worked closely with the World Health Organization and other international groups to institute and maintain preventive measures and to educate the public at all levels using a variety of platforms. Thailand also made strong efforts to offer remuneration to farmers who had lost income and poultry due to the disease.

In December 2004 disaster struck in the form of a tsunami triggered by an earthquake beneath the Indian Ocean. Much of southern Thailand was destroyed, with approximately 5,400 people dead and more than 2,800 missing in Thailand, many of them tourists.

In the parliamentary elections of 6 February 2005, Thaksin's party won 376 out of 500 seats, the first time any party had ever won an absolute majority. Thaksin also made history as the first prime minister to serve two consecutive terms in office. His popularity surged in part due to his effective handling of the tsunami crisis. Then, in July 2005, Thaksin declared a state of emergency to contain violence in the southern states of Pattani, Yala and Narathiwat. These predominantly Muslim provinces had repeatedly launched military assaults and arson attacks on schools since the start of 2004. In February 2007 about 30 coordinated bombs went off at bars, hotels and electrical installations in Thailand. Although many commentators criticised Thaksin for harsh tactics that did little to curb insurgency in the south, he enjoyed a strong base of rural support.

In 2006 Thaksin's family earned almost US$ 2 billion from the sale of assets in their telecommunications company. Thaksin faced public discontent over his handling of Muslim insurgents, as well as serious allegations of tax evasion and corruption; demonstrations in Bangkok demanded the resignation of Thaksin and two of his cabinet ministers. Facing mounting criticism, Thaksin dissolved parliament in late February and called for early elections in April, after which he resigned in protest despite winning 57 per cent of the votes.

On 19 September 2006, while Thaksin was in New York City for a meeting of the United Nations General Assembly, a bloodless coup was held in Bangkok and the military declared martial law. General (retired) Surayud Chulanont was sworn in as prime minister in October 2006, with promises of new general elections to be held late in 2007 following the drafting of a new constitution. A constitutional court found the Thai Rak Thai Party of former prime minister Thaksin Shinawatra guilty of a fraudulent April 2006 election. The party was prohibited from participation in government for five years.

Elections were held in Thailand in December 2007. Samak Sundaravej and his People's Power Party (PPP) was declared winners with 228 seats of the possible 480 seats in the House.

TRADITIONS

THAI SYMBOLS

The Ratchaphruek (Golden Shower)—the Thai National Flower

The *ratchaphruek* (*Cassia fistula Linn*) tree bears clusters of beautiful yellow flowers. In Thailand, yellow is regarded as the colour of Buddhism as well as of Thai royalty. *Ratchaphruek* flowers bloom annually from February to May, at which time the tree sheds its foliage and the golden blooms are prominently displayed on the branches, with hardly any leaf. The tree also has a ritual importance because the tree trunk is used as part of the foundation-laying ceremony for buildings. The root, bark, leaves and seeds of the tree are also used in herbal medicines. The *ratchaphruek* is widely known in Thailand and grows in abundance along the roadsides.

The Chang (Elephant)

The elephant is considered Thailand's national animal. It has historically played a pivotal role in the livelihood, customs and transportation of the Thai people. It is also highly respected as a symbol of peace, wisdom, strength and longevity. An elephant with raised trunk symbolises the overcoming of barriers in one's path.

The white elephant, in particular, has long been a sacred animal and a royal symbol included in court celebrations and ceremonies. White is considered a colour of power, purity and light. Legend has it that at the birth of the Buddha, his mother dreamt of a white elephant offering her a lotus flower. One Ayutthayan king, Cakkraphat (r. 1548–1569), is said to have captured more than nine white elephants during his reign.

In Siam, laws were passed that any white elephants found had to be offered to the Siamese king. Senior officials cared for the animals fastidiously and they were kept within the confines of the palace grounds. The death of a white elephant was regarded as an omen of misfortune or tragedy.

Featured on the Siamese national flag until 1917, the white elephant is widely represented in sculptures, paintings, woodcarvings and murals throughout Thailand today.

The Dok-Bua (Lotus Flower)

The *dok-bua* (lotus flower) is found growing in the muddy water of ponds and lakes throughout Thailand. The Thai people treasure it as a symbol of beauty that is created or rises out of dirt. It also is the traditional flower of Buddhism; Buddhists believe that the Buddha could walk at birth and that lotus flowers bloomed to cushion his feet at his first seven steps. The flower also has medicinal value and is an ingredient in oils, creams and lotions. The large lotus leaf is often used to wrap cooked food.

The Crown Chakra (the energy at the top of one's head) is often called the Thousand-Petal Lotus, the symbol of final revelation. In Buddhism, an opened lotus possesses a solar disposition; the flower is associated with the sun's rays and is itself a representation of enlightenment. It is said that meditating on the lotus brings harmony to all facets of one's being.

PHRA PHUM CHAOTHI (THE SPIRIT HOUSE)

Seen throughout Thailand are small houses believed to shelter spirits that "protect" the home and property of Thai people. Typically made of wood, brick or concrete and positioned on a raised platform or pillar for a good vantage point, the *phra phum chaothi*, or Thai spirit house, ranges in size and style, from miniature traditional northern Thai houses, palaces and Khmer-inspired structures to large buildings into which one can walk. Spirit houses are often adorned with human and animal figurines, and perhaps even with tiny furniture. Incense, candles, flowers and food are usually placed on the porch as offerings. Each day the owners of the house perform an offering ceremony asking for happiness, prosperity and blessings.

Thai folklore includes many gods and celestial beings, but the *phra phum,* or Guardian Spirits of the Land, are regarded as the most important. There are nine types of Guardian Spirits, including the Guardian of the House and the Guardian of Gardens. The remaining seven types of spirits protect other natural and human-made objects, from forests and mountains to storehouses and military defences. The spirits can be good or evil, and humans are expected to keep them informed of important events, such as the start of a new business or project. Failure to show such respect may result in misfortune.

One of Thailand's more famous spirit houses is the Chiang Mai City Pillar in northern Thailand. People visit this spirit house with offerings to ask for very large requests, usually on behalf of a big group. Visitors to Thailand often purchase small spirit houses as mementoes. They are produced in the Bangkok and Ayutthaya provinces and in northern Thailand.

SALA THAI

The word *sala* is Pali (the ancient language of Theravada Buddhism) for pavilion. Traditionally an open-sided building with a multi-tiered roof and a *prasat* (spire) on the top, the Thai pavilion is the architectural symbol of Thailand and common throughout the country. Many courtyards of *wat* have pavilions for shelter, where people may meditate, eat, rest or read. The Aisawan Thippa at the centre of the pond at the Bang Pa-In Summer Palace in Ayutthaya Province is a well-known example of *sala* architecture.

THAI TRADITIONAL MASSAGE

In Thailand, the ancient skill of traditional massage is regarded as a medical science and part of a holistic approach to healing that supports the body's natural healing process.

Traditional massage can be traced back to 7th-century medical texts written in Pali, the classical language of Theravada Buddhism. Many ancient

Siamese texts were lost when the Burmese destroyed the capital of Ayutthaya in 1767. Those that survived the attack were referred to and reproduced in stone carvings when King Rama II commissioned the epigraphs at Wat Po in Bangkok in the 1820s. These diagrams are an important source of practical information on *nuad boran* (the healing arts) for scholars and therapists. In 1836, King Rama II directed the gathering of knowledge—pictures and texts in different media and formats—on Thai traditional massage, the medical sciences and pharmacology. The entire collection was housed at Wat Po. Court doctors during the reign of King Rama VI reviewed and translated ancient Sanskrit and Pali medical texts into Thai.

The centres of learning for Thai massage have always been temples, especially since massage, in easing body aches and mental stress, is considered a means of attaining inner tranquility. Today, the Wat Po Thai Traditional Medical School in Bangkok offers courses in traditional massage. Skilled therapists there also offer massage sessions. Thai massage concentrates on the energy that flows along designated channels or *sen* in the human body. Using a combination of reflexology, stretching and the application of varying degrees of pressure, therapists focus on energy points in order to alleviate blockages and restore imbalances in the *sen*.

TRADITIONAL THAI MEDICINE AND HERBS

The earliest mention of herbal medicine in Thailand is a treatise on the medicinal attributes of herbs, in the 13th-century Sukhothai work *The Trilogy of Phra Ruang*. From the Ayutthaya period (17th century), the oldest text on herbs is the King Narai Manuscript. Neither the Wat Po manuals (the collection of ancient medical texts housed at Wat Po since the 19th century) nor the King Narai Manuscript has been fully translated into English. As a result, many experts believe there is still much to learn and understand about Thai traditional medicine.

HEALING HERBS

Some commonly used herbs and spices have known medicinal and cosmetic properties. Turmeric is a main ingredient in Thai healing.

Externally it is applied as an astringent and used in cosmetics. When crushed into a mixture, it is a wonderful moisturiser. Turmeric is also consumed to treat stomach ailments.

Galanga looks a bit like ginger and used in Thai cooking to flavour soups and curries. In traditional medicine it is used to treat digestive and skin ailments. In spa treatments, it is an ingredient in herbal body masks and scrubs.

Tamarind is used in cooking, but components of the plant serve a variety of purposes. The bark is used as an astringent. The flowers are used to lower blood pressure, and the fruit itself has laxative properties. It is a natural exfoliant and is used in cosmetics to smoothen and beautify the skin.

Lemongrass is a herb with a tangy flavour. In traditional Thai medicine it is used for skin problems and headaches. It is valued for its aromatic stress-relieving properties. It is also an effective insect repellent.

Garlic is used extensively in Thai cooking. It is believed to lower cholesterol and act as a diuretic.

Today, Thailand boasts a modern Western medical care system, but Thai traditional healing is also practised throughout the country, especially in the rural countryside. Utilising a holistic approach, traditional Thai healing includes a combination of herbal medicine, massage and meditation. Because there was little communication among Thai traditional medical practitioners of different regions in the past, each region developed unique healing techniques and names and categories of medicine over the years. There have been attempts to integrate Western medicine with Thai traditional medicine, and herbal clinics dispense well-established traditional remedies, sometimes in tandem with Western treatments. The government now requires all formally trained, licenced Thai traditional physicians to undergo three years of training based on a standardised curriculum. At the end of this period of study (or at the end of an optional fourth year studying either traditional midwifery or massage), students must pass an examination set by the Ministry of Public Health.

PHRA PIM (THAI AMULETS) AND CHARMS

Although the majority of people in Thailand believe in Buddhism, animism (the belief that natural objects possess spirits or souls) is a powerful influence in daily life. Archaeological excavations, notably in Sukhothai, unearthed votive tablets—small icons made of clay or precious metals impressed with the image of the Buddha. These tablets were found in the most sacred sections of the temple complexes, the caves used for meditation.

Close to the end of the 19th century, people began treating the votive tablets as amulets and collecting them. Aside from their antique value, it was commonly thought that the amulets were made from clay containing the cremated remains of some of the most revered monks, giving them unique and exceptional power.

The amulets sold today evolved from the votive tablets of old and typically feature an image of the Buddha or a highly respected Buddhist monk. They are made from metals such as copper, silver, gold and ivory, and may even be adorned with precious stones. Apart from protecting the wearer from the actions of malevolent spirits, the amulets are believed to convey blessings, such as boosting popularity, business success or good health. The amulets are hung on a gold chain and worn around the neck, more commonly by men than women.

Amulets sell well in Thailand. In Bangkok, one of the biggest amulet 'markets' is the area around Wat Mahathat near the Grand Palace. Depending on the age, condition, market demand and the personage who created or blessed the amulet, pieces range from the very inexpensive to those commanding rare-antique prices.

PHUANG MALAI (GARLANDS)

Just about everywhere along the roadsides in Bangkok—even at the traffic lights—are street vendors selling *phuang malai* (garlands). Taxi drivers hang them from their rear-view mirrors to scent their vehicles, and for their passengers to enjoy. The garlands also have a place in the Buddhist temple tradition and are frequently presented to Buddha images and at shrines as offerings. More intricate and beautiful garlands are sometimes presented to the Thai royal family and other honoured guests.

Flowers used for the garlands include jasmine, marigolds, gardenias and rose petals. The 'basic' garland traditionally has two parts strung with flowers—the circle where the flowers are threaded and the tassels that hang from it. To make the garland, the flowers are pierced with a very long, thin needle and then threaded and formed into a circle.

SAI SIN (SACRED THREAD)

The *sai sin*, or sacred thread, is a ball of unspun white cotton blessed by a monk and used for Buddhist ceremonies. When monks are called upon to bless a house, the thread is placed on a tray in front of an altar. The monks begin chanting and as they continue, the head monk undoes the thread and lets it pass through his fingers. Without breaking the chain, it travels to the next monk and the next until the thread encompasses the perimeter of the structure being blessed. The chanting and blessing by each monk in turn ensures that a sacrosanct circle has been formed and all within its boundaries will be protected from evil and harm.

The sacred thread is also used at the monks' pre-ordination ceremony, when it is tied around the aspirant's wrist for protection against bad spirits and misfortune prior to being ordained. People of northern and northeastern Thailand believe that a length of sacred thread tied around a visitor's wrists can protect him or her from harm and evil spirits. A special ceremony called Bai Si Su Khwan or Tham Khwan is performed when a person has been sick or has gone through particularly difficult times. The master of the ceremony ties the *sai sin* around the wrists of the subject and of the family or community members assembled for the occasion. As part of the ceremony, the sacred thread is believed to renew the person's vigour for life and give him or her strength.

SAK YANT (TRADITIONAL TATTOOS)

Tattoos done by Buddhist monks in the temple are an ancient tradition of Buddhism thought to pre-date the religion itself and to have roots in shamanistic magic. The geometric designs and motifs of these tattoos are considered to have magical powers of protection, and they are interwoven with prayers written in the ancient Pali script.

Body tattoos are made using Indian ink, but tradition often dictates the inclusion of other 'magical' components in the ink, such as lizard skin or snake venom! The monks use tools such as sharpened bamboo sticks or thin, weighted metal rods to draw the tattoos. Traditionally, these tattoos were sported by Thai fighters. It was believed that the tattooed *yant* designs protected the fighter against weapons—that his body would be too slick for a weapon to pierce his skin.

RELIGION

Approximately 90 per cent of the population in Thailand practises Theravada Buddhism. Muslims form the second largest group. There are also Christians, Sikhs, Hindus and other religious groups in Thailand. Religious freedom is protected in Thailand, and one may practise a religion in peace as long as its practice does not compromise good ethical behaviour, public order or one's civic responsibilities. The Thai Constitution specifies that Thai citizens be endowed with religious freedom and mandates that Thai kings must be Buddhists, but that the king must be the "Upholder of All Religions".

BUDDHISM

The tenets and principles of the Buddhist religion are entwined with Thai culture, tradition and politics. Some commentators have attributed Thailand's political independence and strength to the Buddhist beliefs of its leaders and people.

Siddhartha Gautama, the founder of Buddhism, was born a prince in India between the 6th and 4th centuries BC. Giving up his wealth and royal privileges, he spent his lifetime seeking enlightenment. He studied with gurus, lived as an ascetic for a period, practised intense meditation, trained disciples and established the Sangha, the world's oldest monastic order. Buddhism is based on the teachings of Siddhartha Gautama, or Lord Buddha. Today, Buddhism has two main sects, the Theravada and Mahayana schools.

Unlike the Mahayana, who revere numerous buddhas and bodhisattvas, Theravada Buddhists stress the importance of monastic life and revere only Lord Buddha.

It is not known exactly when Buddhism was founded in Thailand, but it is believed that Theravada Buddhist missionaries directed by the Venerable Sona and Uttara (learned Buddhist monks) under the patronage of Buddhist Indian Emperor Asoke visited what is now Myanmar (Burma) and Nakhon Pathom in the 3rd century BC.

Buddhist dogma consists fundamentally of the Four Noble Truths, as taught by Lord Buddha: *dukha*, or suffering; *samudaya*, or the cause of suffering; *nirvana*, or the cessation of suffering; and *marga*, the path to the end of suffering. Buddhism notes that suffering is a certainty in life. Besides the pain involved in birth, sickness, disappointment, discouragement, grief, aging, despair and death, suffering also includes having contact with the unpleasant, losing contact with the pleasant and being unable to attain one's desires. Buddhism teaches that one must first recognise that suffering is caused by desire (lust, greed for wealth or power) and that nirvana is attainable through our own willpower and self-control; we do not need gods or priests to conduct us. Lord Buddha himself claimed to have attained full enlightenment, a state of perfect non-suffering and non-existence, and thereby to have been freed from future reincarnation.

According to the Buddhist doctrine of *karma*, the doing of good deeds is rewarded with a tendency towards similar good deeds, while the committing of bad deeds gives rise to a tendency towards similar bad deeds, either in the present life or in a future incarnation. "Making merit" or doing good deeds is therefore an important part of the Buddhist life. In Thailand, examples of "making merit" include giving food to the monks who make their neighbourhood rounds collecting alms in the early morning. People also donate religious articles to monasteries; the wealthier the community, the more expensive and imposing the donated objects.

It is common for a young Thai male to undertake vows of temporary monkhood before the age of 18. This act brings merit to the entire family. The young men remain monks for a period ranging from only a few days to several months. As novices, they learn about Buddhist history and philosophy, the path to enlightenment and meditation techniques.

The Annual Rains Retreat, a period of about three months between July and October coinciding with the monsoon season and associated with spiritual renewal, is a popular time for young men to undertake temporary vows to be ordained as Buddhist monks. His Majesty King Bhumibol Adulyadej and Crown Prince Maha Vajiralongkorn both were monks for short periods of time.

Buddhist Monks

The Mahanikai (wearing orange robes), and the Thammayut (wearing dark red robes) are the two types of Buddhist monks found in Thailand. The Thammayut are the more conservative; strict adherents to the tenets of academic Buddhism, they eat only one meal a day and are not permitted to touch money.

Monks are an integral part of Thai life and are called upon to participate in ceremonies and rituals such as the blessing of new houses, offices and cars. Buddhist monks are highly respected not only for their disciplined lives but also because they represent a spirit of goodness. They practice chastity, self-discipline and social good, and their keen insight into religious and spiritual practices and philosophies is highly revered. Out of respect for the monks and for their moral purity, interaction between monks and women are highly controlled; they are not permitted to interact in private, and a monk may not touch an object that is being or has been held by a woman. A woman makes her offerings by placing them on a receiving cloth on the floor before the monk. She must never touch the alms bowl, stand too close to a monk or touch a monk's robe.

The status of a monk is dependent on his seniority and administrative or social responsibilities, and he can be elevated to a higher position in acknowledgement of his service. The abbot has the ultimate power within the *wat* and determines administrative, clerical, disciplinary and social responsibilities and actions within the *wat* and in the community. People may seek moral, spiritual or personal guidance from senior monks and abbots. A marriage must be presided over by nine monks, and the ritual chanting at the three-day duration of a funeral must be performed by a group of monks.

Theravada Buddhist nuns are women who practise the precepts (laws of conduct and lifestyle) of Buddhism and have adopted an ascetic lifestyle. As a religious order they enjoy the royal patronage of the queen of Thailand. They wear white robes and live at home, in temples or in nunneries. Besides devotion to prayer and good works, the nuns' daily activities include cooking, cleaning, washing and maintaining the temple grounds.

A MONK'S LIFE

A Buddhist monk abides by the Patimokkha Rules, the basic Theravada code of 227 rules governing all aspects of life, including dietary restrictions, sexual celibacy, moral conduct and the treatment of material possessions. A monk is permitted to have eight essential items: three robes, a bowl for alms, a knife, a needle, a waistband and a water strainer. Other items can be received as offerings from the monk's followers. A typical morning for a monk may include waking up at 4:00 am for prayer, accepting alms offerings from lay followers and returning to the temple for breakfast, followed by more prayers. The monk is customarily allowed time for study or other activities. Lunch is usually at 11:00 am, and the afternoon is spent on other duties and responsibilities either within the *wat* or outside, such as performing marriages or offering blessings.

SACRED WATER

Lustral water is water that has been blessed by monks at a ceremony and is used for sacred occasions. Lustral water is prepared from rainwater or groundwater. As monks chant prayers and drip wax from a lit candle into the water, it is believed that evil, sickness and misfortune are washed away and the water becomes holy. Lustral water is contained in a special container or an alms bowl on the altar. Thais believe that drinking it or having it sprinkled on the head will bring blessings of good fortune, security and prosperity.

The Buddhist Wat

Approximately 27,000 Buddhist *wat* (temples or monasteries) are scattered throughout the country. The *wat* is traditionally the focal point of diverse activities in a village or community. Although the *wat* is a Buddhist institution, it includes many representative spiritual and historical elements encompassing Hindu and animist beliefs. Architecturally, the *wat* consists of a compound of buildings without any proscribed design or pattern. The largest, central building is called the *viharn*. It contains a Buddha statue (Buddha images are traditionally east-facing) situated in front of a large area open to the general public. It is here that people come to pray and talk with the monks. Murals showing the various stages of the Buddha's life typically adorn the temple walls. During festivals and merit-making activities, the *wat* becomes a social centre for people of all ages. One must be properly (and respectfully) attired when visiting temples; shorts, sleeveless shirts and rubber-thonged footwear are considered inappropriate.

On one side of the *viharn* are *chedi,* conical structures painted either white or gold. They contain the relics or remains of religious leaders. A Thai may request that after death and cremation his/her ashes be enshrined in a small *chedi*. The *bot* is the ordination hall of the wat, an area marked out by eight black stones, where new monks take their vows and other rituals and religious ceremonies take place. The *wat* frequently includes a library on the grounds, usually a carved wooden building on a raised platform, where education and learning occurs. It is also customary to have a *bodhi* tree (a specimen of tree easily recognised by its heart-shaped leaves) on the grounds because the Buddha sat under this tree the night he attained enlightenment. The monks who live in the *wat* sleep in separate lodgings called *kuti*, and it is the responsibility of the monks to manage, clean, watch over, teach and meditate in the *wat*.

Temple buildings are usually covered with small, reflective pieces of coloured glass to ward off evil spirits using the spirits' own frightening reflections. Other representations to scare away evil spirits include 'monster' figures posted to guard entryways and the *naga,* a multi-headed serpent who guarded the Buddha during his meditations. The scaly backs of *naga* form the handrails of staircases, and the candleholders by the altar are usually made in the shape of *naga.* This legendary serpent is a symbol of security and comfort in Thailand.

Temples also feature many images of the Buddha. Smaller statues may be made of bronze, brass or gold; larger statues are covered in cement or stucco (an exterior finish of fine plaster or other decorative material). All Buddha images are sacrosanct in Thailand. The main Buddha image in a temple will have many offerings in front of it, including flowers (especially lotus blossoms), money trees and small statues.

Buddhist Holidays

Buddhist holidays are considered national holidays.

Asanha Puja

Celebrated on the 15th day of the eighth lunar month, this holiday marks the day when Lord Buddha gave his first sermon to his first disciples upon their attaining enlightenment.

Khao Phansa

Khao Phansa, or Buddhist Lent, is the three-month period from the first day of the eighth lunar month to the 15th day of the eleventh lunar month. It coincides with the rainy season or Annual Rains Retreat in Thailand and is celebrated in remembrance of Lord Buddha's instruction that monks remain in one location to study and meditate during the rainy season. Lay Buddhist followers make offerings of clothing, medicine and Lenten candles for the monks to use during their retreat.

Thot Kathin

During Khao Phansa, the assembly of monks identifies the most disciplined monks with the oldest robes. At the end of Buddhist Lent, these monks are presented with new *kathin,* or robes, in a joyful and colourful ceremony called Thot Kathin. The donation of *kathin* robes to the monks is an opportunity for lay Buddhists to make much merit, and this is a very popular holiday, with lots of food and entertainment.

Magha Puja

Celebrated on the day when the moon is at its fullest in the third lunar month, Magha Puja honours the day of the Fourfold Assembly, when four events occurred simultaneously: the gathering of 1250 monks before Lord Buddha, all of whom had achieved the status of enlightened beings, all of whom had been individually ordained by the Lord Buddha himself, and all on the day of the full moon in the month of Magha.

Visakha Puja

Observed on the full moon day of the sixth lunar month, Visakha Puja commemorates Lord Buddha's birth, enlightenment and passing. Buddhists throughout Thailand earn merit by donating food to monks, praying, and giving offerings of flowers, candles and incense. An elaborate ceremony is held at Phuttha Monthon (near Bangkok) in the province of Nakhon Pathom at the statue of the 'walking' Buddha. A member of the royal family leads the procession here, and worshippers from surrounding areas participate in meditation and prayer.

ISLAM

A little over 6 per cent of the Thai population is Muslim. Malay Muslims living in the southern provinces of Yala, Narathiwat, Satun and Pattani speak the Malay language and form the majority (about 70 per cent) of Thailand's Muslim population. The remaining Thai Muslims are non-Malay and originate from various countries, including Iran, Cambodia, Pakistan, India, China and, more recently, the Arab world.

Although the southern Malay kingdoms have been under strong Thai influence since the 16th century, they did not officially become part of Thailand until 1902. The Thai government attempted in the 1930s and 1940s to absorb and nationalise the southern Muslim community, for instance, by changing the language of instruction in their traditional schools from Malay-Arabic to Thai. These efforts were met with great dissatisfaction among the southern Muslims, who found security and sanctuary in their identity and Islamic beliefs. Periodic outbreaks of violence characterise the relationship between the Government and militant separatist elements in the southern provinces.

Islam is the world's second largest religion after Christianity, with well over one billion adherents to the faith. Although Muslims may live in different parts of the world, they share a common belief in one God called Allah. Islam began more than 1400 years ago when it was disclosed in Mecca, Arabia. Muslims believe that Allah sent prophets to humankind to teach them His will. The last of these messengers was the 6th-century prophet Muhammad, and the religion of Islam dates from his time. The laws of Islam are contained in the Qur'an.

Every Muslim is expected to live by the Five Pillars of Islam: *shahadah* (the Muslim profession of faith); *salat* (ritual prayers performed five times daily); *zakat* (the giving of alms to support the poor and destitute); *sawam* (fasting during Ramadan); and *hajj* (the major pilgrimage to Mecca).

Like Thai Buddhism, Islam in Thailand has become integrated with practices and beliefs not traditionally found in Islam, for instance with animist customs of the indigenous Malay culture. Most of the country's mosques are associated with the Sunni branch of Islam. A small number of mosques are of the Shi'ite minority. Shi'ite Muslims believe that Muslim leaders must be descended from the family of Muhammad alone, whereas Sunnite Muslims accept other reasonable claims to leadership. Sunnites regard their sect as the mainstream branch of Islam.

Islamic education in Thailand is based on the *pondok* (private Islamic schools) and is important to the Malay-Muslim community in Thailand, providing religious teaching and an understanding of the community. About 500 *pondok* operate in southern Thailand, the smallest numbering only a handful of students. Tok Guru are the religious teachers and heads of the schools. Students learn the Qur'an, basic Arabic and tenets of Islam. Many *pondok* have also integrated secular and vocational subjects into the syllabus.

Special legal provisions are in place to support Islam in Thailand, including a royal decree on religious patronage of the religion of Islam and the provision of a National Council for Muslims in Thailand.

SIKHISM

The Sikhs in Thailand are concentrated primarily in Bangkok, but there are about 17 *gurdwara* (Sikh places of worship) throughout the country, including the main ones in Bangkok. *Gurdwara* are also located in Chiang Mai, Cholburi (Pattaya), Khon Kaen, Lampang, Nakhom Ratchasima and Phuket. Sikhism focusses strongly on a mutual sense of cooperation, and a *gurdwara* provides a place for Sikhs to perform prayers and ceremonies as a community. The *gurdwara* also represents a path towards the Gurus, the founder of the movement and his nine successors. Sikhs believe the Gurus were all inhabited by a single spirit, the Spirit of the Eternal Guru, which passed into the Sikh Holy Book, or the Guru Granth Sahib, after the death of the 10th Guru.

Sikhism was founded in the 15th century by Sri Guru Nanak Dev Ji in the Punjab, India. Sikhs believe in One Supreme God (Vahiguru) whose purpose is to enable humans to realise their purpose in the universe. Sikhs are committed to the teachings of the Gurus as contained in the Sikh Holy Book. The five basic vices are lust, anger, greed, pride, and ego, and a person is considered God-conscious if he or she does not lapse into these immoralities. Humans must free themselves from the cycle of reincarnation by letting go of self-centredness and accepting God-centredness. Sikhs are also expected to recite five prayers daily, meditate in the name of God, earn a fair livelihood and fight for justice in the name of humanity and peace.

HINDUISM

Hinduism is a combination of beliefs, customs and ancient legends, with a history pre-dating 3000 BC. Many Hindus acknowledge Brahma as the one God, with numerous other gods and goddesses as his different articulations. There is, however, a diversity of views regarding the deities within Hinduism itself. The three principal gods are Brahma (creator of the universe), Vishnu (preserver of the universe) and Shiva (destroyer of the universe). Vishnu (also called Narayana) is worshipped as the greatest of the gods, appearing on earth to rescue mankind from oppression or physical disasters. Numerous lesser gods exist.

Hinduism reached Thailand more than 2,000 years ago. Today there are approximately 100,000 Hindus in Thailand, most of whom are businesspeople who have actively preserved their culture, customs and way of life. Many aspects of Hinduism are deeply ingrained in Thai society and culture: the Dharmasastras (Hindu scriptures), Hindu deities, Hindu idea of kingship and Hindu literature and festivals. Thai rulers have used Hindu brahmins (priests) to participate and perform rituals, including blessings by Hindu deities. When a new building is blessed, Hindu deities are worshipped along with the Buddha and Thai spirits. One of the most popular shrines in Bangkok, the Hindu Erawan shrine, houses a statue of four-faced Brahma, the Hindu god of creation. Thai ceremonies follow the precepts of the Shatapatha Brahmana and the Aitareya Brahmana, prose texts describing Vedic ritual and history. (The Vedas are the oldest sacred texts of Hinduism.) Archaeological excavations in Thailand have uncovered icons of Hindu gods and goddesses, and sculptures of the Hindu gods—Parvati, Hanuman, Ganesh, Vishnu and Brahma—decorate Thai temple walls throughout the country. The Hindu god Vishnu's birdlike mount *garuda* is also the royal symbol in Thailand.

There are four main Hindu temples in Bangkok, located in neighbourhoods where most of the Hindu community lives. Hindu worship involves making personal offerings to the deities at shrines that often feature images or representations of the deities. Visitors to the temples are often Thai Buddhists as well as Hindus. Thais have a deep understanding of and respect for the connections between Hinduism and Buddhism. Many Thai people who are not Hindu go to specific Hindu gods to pray. Thais may be followers of the Hindu god Brahma, for instance, because it was Brahma who offered guidance to the Buddha. In addition, there are many similarities between Thai festivals and Hindu festivals in Thailand.

CHRISTIANITY

In 1567, Dominican missionaries Jeronimo da Cruz and Sebastiâo da Canto arrived in Ayutthaya to introduce Roman Catholicism to Thailand. They were later joined by American and European Presbyterians, Baptists and Seventh Day Adventists. Most converts came from the immigrant Chinese population, with only a small number of Thai converts. Less than one per cent of the population of Thailand is Christian.

During the reign of King Rama III (1824–1851), missionary doctors arrived in Thailand. Among them was Dr. Dan Beach Bradley, an American Protestant missionary widely acknowledged for his contributions to Thailand. During his 35 years in the country, Bradley taught Christianity, founded the first printing press in Bangkok, performed the first modern medical operation in Thailand and introduced the smallpox vaccination. He also built the first dispensary, which became the prototype for clinics throughout the country.

Christian missionary groups throughout Thailand have built and supported clinics, schools, hospitals and universities, working extensively to improve education and public health particularly among the northern hill tribes.

ANIMISM

Animism is considered one of the earliest forms of religion, with roots in prehistoric times. Animism recognises that humans share the universe with a spiritual realm and that all natural objects—plants, animals and celestial bodies—have spirits.

Although Buddhism is not an animistic religion, many elements of indigenous animist beliefs can be recognised in Thai rituals and ceremonies. The spirit house is one good example of the way Buddhism has fused with animism in Thailand. Northern hill tribes such as the Yao continue to adhere to customs and beliefs that are largely animistic.

TAOISM (DAOISM)

Taoism is the religion of a very small minority in Thailand. The religion was founded by Lao-Tzu, a 6th-century Chinese philosopher and contemporary of Confucius. His classic, *Tao-te Ching* (*Of the Way of Power*), resulted from his search for a system of beliefs to stop the conflicts and wars during his lifetime. The Tao ("The Way") began as a blend of psychology and philosophy but became a state religion in China in AD 440. Taoism stresses harmony with nature and includes the practices of meditation, Chinese geomancy, fortune-telling and the chanting of scriptures. There is no supreme being, but Taoists may worship a hierarchy of deities and ancestral spirits.

PEOPLE AND
LANGUAGES

TRADITIONAL REGIONS

The five historical regions of Thailand are Lanna Thai (northern Thailand); Isan (northeastern Thailand); the Central Plain; Pak Tai (southern Thailand); and western and southwestern Thailand.

The people of the Lanna Thai region speak a dialect of the Thai language called Kham Mu'ang, or Yuan. The region is also home to some of the tribal groups who have migrated over the years from Myanmar, Laos and southern China. The people of the Isan region share many of the cultural characteristics of the Lao people living in Laos across the Mekong River, including the regional dialect called Lao. The people of this region have been comparatively autonomous until the 18th century, and their identity is somewhat unique from that of Thai in the rest of Thailand.

Most of the Chao Phraya River basin is situated in the Central Plain. The people here are called Siamese and speak Standard Thai, the national language of Thailand. Bangkok, one of Asia's most important urban centres, is located in this region, making it a heavily populated area with significant industrial and commercial activity. The coastal region from Bangkok to the Cambodian border is home to a large population of Chinese descent. During the late 19th century, many Chinese immigrants settled here to work in sugarcane plantations, lumber mills and small business operations. People along the border of Cambodia speak Khmer and practice Khmer cultural traditions.

Together with the Central Plain, the Pak Tai region in southern Thailand, specifically Nakhon Si Thammarat, played a significant role in the history of the country. As a result of a common cultural and historical heritage, the language and customs of this region resemble those of central Thailand. The southernmost areas close to northern Malaysia are predominantly Muslim and Malay-speaking.

Western and southwestern Thailand bordering Myanmar is thinly populated. The terrain is hilly and mountainous. The Karen hill tribe group has settlements here.

DEMOGRAPHY

Thailand's population numbers a little over 64 million (2003 estimate). Ethnic Thais make up 75 per cent of the population, Chinese 14 per cent, and other ethnicities (Malay, Indian, Mon, Khmer, hill minorities etc.) approximately 11 per cent. The literacy rate (as of 2003) is 96 per cent.

The capital and the country's largest city is Bangkok, with an estimated population of 6.6 million (2003 estimate) within the city limits. Migration to Bangkok from outlying provinces has contributed to its development as a crowded commercial centre.

The Thai population surged between 1950 and 1970, but growth has since slowed due to private family planning options and official strategies in place. Many other Asian countries wishing to curb their population expansion have looked to Thailand as a model.

Since the 1960s and 1970s, Thailand has received many political refugees from Cambodia and Vietnam, including Hmong refugees, who settled along the Thai border following the Vietnam War.

HILL GROUPS

Thailand's cultural minorities, the hill tribes, live in the northern mountains of the country. Over the past two centuries, they have migrated to Thailand from Tibet, Laos, Burma and China. Because their villages are remote and many have little contact with urban areas, only rough estimates exist for the number of tribal groups and the size of their populations. The main groups are the Yao, Karen, Akha, Lahu, Hmong (Meo) and Lisu. In the past, the Hmong, Yao, Lahu and Lisu groups depended on the cultivation of opium for livelihood, these groups now grow crops such as strawberries, coffee, vegetables and flowers.

The Yao (Mien)

The Yao trace their origins to southern China. Today, they live in southern China, Laos, Burma, Vietnam and Thailand. In Thailand, they number about 60,000, located in Nan, Lampang, Chiang Rai, Phayao, Chiang Mai, Phitsanulok and Kamphaeng Phet. Their traditional houses are made of wood or bamboo, with thatched grass roofs. There are separate entrances for men (leading to a guest area) and women (leading to the kitchen), as well as a "big door" used in ceremonies. Opposite this special door is the ancestral altar.

The traditional religion of the Yao is animistic, and today the people practise a blend of Taoism and ancestral worship. Medicine people (or shamans) communicate with the spirit world on behalf of humans. The Yao believe in spirits and amulets of protection. Hats with decorations and dangling silver coins are also used to protect children from evil spirits. The Yao also believe in spirits that bring good fortune and longevity.

The Yao traditional dress in Thailand consists of a black turban, a large red ruffled collar, black jacket and beautiful hand-embroidered loose trousers. An ankle-length embroidered tunic is worn over the trousers. Most of the cloth is black or indigo homespun cotton. Girls learn to embroider at about the age of five. Beautiful hand-embroidered caps are worn by young children.

The Karen (Yang)

The majority of Karen people live in Myanmar, but political conflict in Myanmar has driven some Karen into Thailand since the 18th century. The Karen form the largest tribal group in Thailand, with a population of about 350,000. They consist of four main groups: the White Karen (which in turn consist of the Sgaw and Pwo subgroups), Black Karen, Padung (or Longnecked Karen) and Red Karen. Karen villages are primarily in the northern provinces of Chiang Rai, Chiang Mai and Mae Hong Son, but the tribal group also extends throughout several other provinces.

Although most Karen are concentrated in mountain villages, some also live in lowland plains, towns and valleys. Traditional Karen houses are made of wood or bamboo and stand on stilts. The leader of the village is the village priest, whose responsibility is to maintain the moral conduct of the village and to approve newcomers wishing to become part of the village. The priest also arbitrates disputes and decides when someone must leave because they have violated a taboo or endangered village life.

Karen beliefs are strongly animistic. Land and water spirits must be placated and appeased through prayers and sacrifices, in order for the community and individuals to enjoy good fortune. In recent years, however, Western missionaries have brought Christianity to the Karen, and some have converted.

The Karen are well known for their beautifully woven fabrics and striking traditional dress. Red, white/cream and black colours predominate, and the motifs are primarily geometric. Unmarried girls wear loose V-shaped tunics, and married women wear blouses and skirts. Men wear shirts and loose blue trousers. Traditionally, Karen men adorn themselves with a wide variety and quantity of tattoos on their backs, arms, chests and stomachs.

The Akha

The Akha originated in the Tibetan highlands or in Yunnan, China before they migrated to Burma and then to northern Thailand, establishing the first village in Thailand in 1903, close to the Burmese border. Today, there are about 20,000 Akha living in Thailand.

The Akha typically prefer very high altitudes, building their villages on mountain ridges and slopes that promise fresh drinking water and good farmland. Traditionally the Akha practise animism, but many have now converted to Christianity. The most distinctive characteristics of an Akha village are its ceremonial gates, large village swing and steep rooftops. Houses stand on low stilts. The village gates are decorated with carvings depicting human life, to indicate to spirits that they should not venture into the human domain. The swing is believed to be watched over by guardian spirits.

The group has distinguished and interesting traditional costumes. They wear unique silver headdresses and black clothes with beautifully and uniquely embroidered jackets. Clothing is beaded and generously embellished with silver ornaments and buttons.

The Lahu (Musur)

The Lahu originated on the Tibetan planes, migrated to southwestern China and travelled southwards, some settling in Laos, Myanmar, Vietnam and Thailand. In northern Thailand today, they number about 80,000 scattered across the provinces of Khampeng Phet, Mae Hong Son, Chiang Rai and Chiang Mai.

The Lahu are divided into several subgroups, of which about six live in Thailand. The largest Lahu group in Thailand is the Red Lahu. The women of this group wear black trousers and red and blue striped sleeves. Women of the Black Lahu group wear black cloaks with diagonal cream stripes and sleeves striped in red and yellow. Men of both groups wear Chinese-style cropped trousers.

The Lahu live at high altitudes. Houses are built on tall stilts, with a fireplace in the centre where family members gather. The traditional beliefs are animistic, and when a house is built, a ceremony is performed and beeswax candles lit in order to drive out any spirits that might have arrived along with the building materials. In recent times, however, many Lahu have converted to Buddhism or Christianity.

In the past, the Lahu were weavers, but many have now lost this art. Embroidery and basket-making are the main crafts of the Lahu, and these are sold in crafts markets throughout Thailand.

The Hmong (Meo)

The majority of the Hmong people still live in China, where they originated. Small communities have migrated as far away as the United States and Europe. In Southeast Asia, the Hmong live in Vietnam, Laos, Myanmar and Thailand, numbering about 130,000 in Thailand. The largest populations are found in Phetchaburi, Chiang Mai, Chiang Rai and Tak.

The Hmong comprise the Blue and White Hmong subgroups. Blue Hmong wear blue pleated batik-patterned skirts with an embroidered and/or and appliquéd border. Jackets are short and typically have a cross-stitched decorative border. White Hmong women usually wear indigo-dyed trousers, reserving plain hemp cloth skirts for ceremonial occasions. Men wear a black decorated jacket with Chinese style three-quarter length trousers. Embroidery adorns the jacket. Silver jewellery is a strong indication of wealth in the Hmong tribal group.

The Hmong live at high altitudes. Unlike other hill tribes, however, their houses are built on the ground and not on stilts. The houses have dirt floors and roofs that slope almost to the ground.

Traditional Hmong beliefs are strongly animistic, and most Hmong have resisted conversion to other religions. Household and ancestral spirits are respected and ceremonies conducted to ask for blessings or protection. One of the most interesting pieces of Hmong jewellery is the 'soul lock'. It is worn to keep the soul in the body.

The Lisu

The Lisu number about 30,000 in Thailand. They originated probably in eastern Tibet, moving to Yunnan, China and arriving relatively late in Thailand, perhaps only about 100 years ago. The Lisu comprise two main groups: the Flowery and the Black Lisu.

The Lisu live at moderate to high altitudes, close to water sources, in bamboo houses built on the ground. Dirt floors surround a central ridge or platform. The Lisu worship ancestral and nature spirits, and shamans consult the spirits when a cure for disease or sickness is needed. Every house has an ancestral altar or small shrine and a spirit house built on posts.

The Lisu traditional garments are extremely colourful. Women wear knee-length tunics over blue or green trousers. Their tops are heavily embroidered with thin bands of red, yellow and blue at the sleeves, shoulders and cuffs. Men wear blue jackets and loose trousers in yellow, green or pink. Festival dress is even more elaborate, with waistcoats and belts in intricate silver designs.

COMMUNICATION

Languages

The shifting of political boundaries over centuries has played a significant role in the varied ethnic, linguistic, religious and cultural combinations within Thailand. Several language families are represented in Thailand, the most historically significant of which is the Tai family of languages (see *History* chapter), spoken by the Tai peoples of the region.

Today, the majority of people throughout Thailand speak the Thai language, the most important language in the Tai family of tongues. These languages are so similar that in general the grammar, structures and other rules of Thai also apply to all the other Tai languages.

Tai languages are tonal, meaning that words of the same sound are differentiated in meaning by various tones. The Tai languages together have as many as nine tones, but Standard Thai (a national standard based on the tongue spoken in Bangkok) has five: level, low, falling, high and rising. In writing, the absence of a diacritic denotes the level tone. Four diacritics denote the remaining tones: the grave accent, as in *màak* (low tone); the circumflex, as in *mâak* (falling tone); the acute accent, as in *máa* (high tone); and the wedge, as in *mǎa* (rising tone). Thus the word *maa* (level tone) means "to come", while *máa* (high tone) means "horse", and *mǎa* (rising tone) means "dog".

Thai vocabulary includes words borrowed from Chinese, Khmer (the national language of Cambodia), Sanskrit, Pali (an ancient Indian language) and, increasingly, English.

THE THAI ALPHABET

> Ramkhamhaeng the Great (c. 1239–1298), the third ruler of the Sukothai Kingdom, is credited with the invention of the Thai alphabet in the late 13th century. The writing system is based on the Indic script and has 44 consonants, in addition to numerous vowels, diphthongs and vowel-consonant combinations. Writing proceeds horizontally from left to right in undivided blocks of letters, with spaces denoting punctuation. When Thai is romanised, it is done so phonetically. A Thai word rendered in the English alphabet may therefore have many different spellings.

The Lao language is closely related to Thai and belongs in the same (Tai) family of languages. Lao speakers live in the Khorat Plateau that is adjacent to Laos, and they make up about a quarter of Thailand's population. The Mon people (originally from Burma) are congregated primarily west of Bangkok, and the Khmer are concentrated mainly along the Cambodian border. Mon and Khmer peoples originally spoke tongues in the Mon-Khmer language group, but most of them in Thailand now speak Standard Thai as their first language.

Speakers of Sino-Tibetan languages, such as the Karen people and other hill tribes, live in the western and northern mountains. The Chinese have a long history in Thailand, and most are concentrated in and around Bangkok and other urban centres. They speak Mandarin and the Chinese dialects but also have a good command of Standard Thai and English. English is taught in schools and understood to varying degrees throughout the country.

Forms of Address

In Thailand, respect is shown for those of a higher status in age, wealth, professional and/or educational qualifications, social status or familial connections. Thais are therefore quite particular about knowing the status of the person they are addressing; what the outsider might regard as an overly curious nature is usually just a means of acquiring sufficient information about a person in order to accord them due respect.

Thais use different forms of address depending on the status of the person they are greeting. Here are just a few examples. *Khun* is a polite generic form of address employed for new acquaintances or people about whom one has insufficient information to use any other title. The term is applicable to either male or female. For instance, a Thai meeting my friend Tessa for the first time might call her *Khun Tessa*. High-ranking government officials may be addressed as *Than*. *Ajarn* is used to address a teacher, for example *Ajarn Richard* or *Ajarn Arthur*.

The Thai Smile

Just about every brochure on Thailand refers to the country as the "land of smiles". Indeed the Thais have made smiling an interpretive art, perfecting creative non-verbal communication. Slight movements of facial features—the mouth, eyes and even the nose—alone or in any combination accompanying a smile can mean much more than simply happiness; smiles can signify states as varied as apology, frustration or annoyance.

A DICTIONARY OF SMILES

The Royal Institute in Thailand was established in 1933 during the reign of King Rama VII (King Prajadhipok) to encourage research and knowledge advantageous to Thailand and other countries and to act in an advisory capacity on academic matters. The Royal Institute's Thai-Thai Dictionary includes a list of the different kinds smiles, or *yim*. Other publications and guides to Thai culture also often describe the varied meanings of Thai smiles. For example, *fuen yim* is a stiff smile such as one might give when a joke is not humorous but a polite response is needed. *Yim thak thaan* is a smile given to encourage the other person to speak even though you dislike his or her idea. *Yim thang nam* is the Thai equivalent of tears of joy–given when the smiler is overcome with emotion, such as at the birth of a new baby. In addition, Thais sometimes smile when a foreigner might think smiling is least appropriate, such as in stressful or uncomfortable situations, to relieve the tension or maintain harmony.

The Wai

The *wai* is a gesture of respect performed by placing the palms of the hands together at chest level and lowering the head, with the elbows firm at the sides of the body. The placement of the head and elbows differentiates the Thai *wai* from the bows in other countries. The *wai* is a gesture of greeting, farewell, prayer or apology. Early in youth, children learn how to perform the *wai*, practising it often as it is traditional for a younger person or someone of lower status to bow to a senior. The senior may acknowledge the gesture with a smile or a nod, say "thank you" or return the *wai* without lowering the head.

LIFESTYLE

The Thai Family

The Thai family is the basic (and perhaps most integral) unit in the country. The family plays a vital role in every aspect of life, including social, ethical and moral roles and responsibilities. It is not uncommon for several generations (and the extended family) to live under the same roof. Children learn the boundaries of acceptable behaviour from their elders. The father is the head of the household, but the mother plays a significant role, traditionally in the area of financial management. Although children are treated with tolerance and leniency, they are taught from a young age to respect their elders. This ethic promotes a sense of responsibility, and grown children are expected to take care of their aged parents. This is regarded as a privilege rather than a burden, because the Thais culturally honour the elderly for imparting wisdom to younger generations.

Village Organisation

Beyond the family and extended family is the village unit. A village consists of numerous households served by a local school and a *wat* (a Buddhist temple or monastery). The community funds the *wat*, which is typically set apart from the community or village by an open field, mainly to afford the monks sufficient privacy and seclusion. The open area also functions as a sports field and a place where village celebrations are held. In urban areas, the local neighbourhood is the equivalent of the village unit.

FOOD

Thai food is known around the world for its unique and flavourful combination of spices and ingredients. Garlic, ginger, chillies, tamarind, coconut, lime juice, lemongrass, coriander, fish sauce and shrimp paste are some of the key ingredients used in Thai cooking.

Curries and Soups

Curry dishes, or *kaeng*, may be prepared with or without coconut milk. The differences between red and green curries are in the kind of chillies and spices that are combined into the chilli paste. *Kaeng khiao wan kai* (green chicken curry) is very popular with visitors to Thailand. *Tom* are soup dishes, including *tom chut* (clear soup), *tom krathi* (soup that includes coconut) and the ever popular *tom yam* (a mixture of vegetables, meat or seafood in a sour and spicy soup).

Other Popular Dishes

Stirfried vegetables (*phat phaek*), fried rice (*khao phat*) and fried noodles (*phat Thai*) are favourite dishes. Papaya salad (*som tam*) is made by adding ground garlic, dried shrimps and chillies to shredded green papaya. Palm sugar, lime juice and fish sauce are added to taste.

Desserts

Thai desserts may be made from sticky rice or coconut milk, coconut, flour or eggs. A favourite is mango and sticky rice, which is a combination of ripe mango and glutinous rice, to which coconut milk and sweetened condensed milk are added. Fruit is also often served as dessert. Mangoes, durians, rambutans, longans, mangosteens and lychees are some of the seasonal fruit, while pineapples, bananas, papayas and jackfruit are available all year.

Rice

Rice is an essential component of the Thai diet. Every meal includes rice, whether fried, boiled or steamed. In the northern and northeastern regions, glutinous or "sticky" rice is more common than steamed rice. In a traditional Thai meal, each person has his or her own serving of rice (*khao*). Accompanying food dishes are placed in the centre of the table.

Records show that rice may have been grown in what is now northeastern Thailand as far back as 5,000 years ago. Today Thailand is one of the world's main exporters of rice, with more than 90 different varieties cultivated. Rice planting begins in May at the start of the rainy season, and is harvested in December when the seeds are mature.

Thais believe that there is a Goddess of Rice who protects and watches over the rice crop and who is prayed to during the Phitee Tham Kwan Khao, or Rice Offering Ceremony. Gifts are offered to the goddess to ensure that the rice crop grows well throughout the year. The goddess is sometimes thanked at the end of a meal.

LITERATURE

ANCIENT LITERATURE: THE RAMAKIEN

The *Ramakien* was developed from the Indian epic *Ramayana,* written by the Indian poet Valmiki more than 2,000 years ago. The traditional story blends adventure, morality, some comedy, and elements of magic and divination. The writing of the first full Thai version of the *Ramayana* was sponsored by King Rama I.

The *Ramakien* revolves around the adventures of Rama (Phra Ram) and his faithful brother Lakshman. An army of monkeys headed by Hanuman the white monkey protects the brothers. Their enemies are led by the demon Ravana (Thotsakan). Phra Ram and his cohort must destroy the demons if humankind and the gods are to live in peace.

The *Ramakien* has a significant place in the culture and traditions of Thailand. On the outer wall of Wat Po in Bangkok is a set of 152 panels depicting scenes from the *Ramakien*. A statue of Thotsakan is among the images of demons guarding the temple. The stories of the *Ramakien* have been adapted into classical Thai dance, drama and puppet and shadow puppet theatre.

POETRY

During the Ayutthaya period, a tradition of poetry developed that encompassed several styles. The oldest form is the *khloong,* a style with strict and elaborate tonal and rhyming constraints. The *rai* is another old form of poetry, often employed in historical records and the listing of laws. Sanskrit verse forms influenced the *chan* and *kaap* styles. The *chan* combines light and heavy syllables organised into set sequences. The *kaap* contains a fixed number of syllables and rhythms. Variations of the *kaap* include the *yaanii* (11 syllables per line), *cha-bang* (16) and *suraangkhanaang* (28).

Sunthorn Phu

Popular Thai poet Sunthorn Phu (1786–1855) exerted a strong influence over literature in Thailand. Educated at a Bangkok monastery, he later joined the government service. Sunthorn Phu led a colourful life that included romantic intrigue and terms of imprisonment when he fell out of court favour. His famous works include *Phra Abhai Mani,* featuring the adventures of two princes in a world of enchantment, and *Nirat Muang Klaeng*, a poem describing his journey to see his estranged father and his love for one of the women at the royal court.

Today, Sunthorn Phu Day is celebrated annually on 26 June. In 1986, UNESCO (the United Nations Educational, Scientific and Cultural Organisation) distinguished him as the People's Poet of Thailand. Unfortunately his works are virtually unknown outside the Thai-speaking world, since little of his work has been translated.

Dr. Montri Umavijani

Montri Umavijani (1941–2006) is remembered as one of Thailand's most original poets. As well as 26 volumes of poetry, he penned numerous translations of Thai works and taught at the universities of Silpakorn, Thammasat and Kasetsart for almost 30 years.

PROSE

Works of the 19th Century

King Rama II is hailed as one of Thailand's great poets. He wrote episodes of the *Ramakien* as well as an epic poem based on a popular romance called *Inao*. He is also famous for his rendition of *Krait'ong*, inspired by the legend of a married man, Krait'ong, who falls in love with a crocodile named Vimala. This version begins where the original legend ends, and is filled with action, moral dilemmas and insight into human relations.

Works of the 20th and 21st Centuries

Kings Rama V and Rama VI were also known for their literary prowess and written contributions to the heritage of Thailand. Famous works by Rama V include *Ngo Pa* and *Klai Ban* (*Far Away from Home*), a collection about the king's trip to Europe in 1906–1907. Among the literary achievements of Rama VI are *Matthana Phata, Phra Non Kham Luang* and numerous patriotic essays.

Although much of Thailand's modern literature has not been translated into other languages, English translations of several novels have been published. These include *Snakes* by Wimon Sainimnuan; *Of Time and Tide* by Atsiri Thammachoat; *Time In A Bottle* by Praphatsorn Seikwikun; and *Mad Dogs and Co.*, *The Judgement* and *Time* by Chart Korbjitti. Short stories in anthologies available in English translation include *A Bamboo Bridge Over Rapids* by Seksan Prasertkul; *The Muzzle* by Suchart Sawatsee; and *A Traffic-Wise Couple* and *Blood Buds* by Sila Khoamchai.

THE SEA WRITE AWARD

The South East Asian Writers Award (SEA Write Award) honours writers and poets from the ASEAN (Association of Southeast Asian Nations) region—Brunei, Cambodia, Indonesia, Laos, Malaysia, Myanmar, the Philippines, Singapore, Thailand and Vietnam. The annual award is presented to a representative from each country, although not every country is represented every year. Initiated in 1979 to recognise the region's literary talent, the award is backed by Thai royal and commercial patronage and support.

The winner of the SEA Write Award for 2006 was Thai writer and translator Ngarmpun Vejjajiva for her novel, *The Happiness of Kati*. Ngarmpun was born to Thai parents in England but moved to Thailand when she was three years old. Prior to writing this first novel, she also wrote short stories for magazines. *The Happiness of Kati* is the story of a young Thai girl mourning the death of her mother and also experiencing life in a small Thai village. The book has been translated into French, English, Japanese and German. Winners of the award in previous years include well-known Thai writers Chart Korbjitti and Wuthichat Choomsanit, whose pen name is Binlah Sonkalagiri.

PROVERBS AND
FOLKLORE

Because Thailand is predominantly Buddhist, many religious proverbs and sayings have made it into everyday speech. 'Folk' proverbs, linked closely to village life and rural occupations, as well as literary proverbs, the most famous being from the *Ramakien*, are also common.

PROVERBS

From the Ramakien

The *Ramakien* is well known to most Thai people because of its deeply embedded historical and cultural roots and its influence on all levels of Thai theatre and society. One proverb, "Crooks as the eighteen coronets", describes Phra Ram's eighteen monkey companions, who often triumph over their demon enemies using trickery. In the *khon* masked drama, all non-human characters wear different types of masks, some with coronets or crowns.

About Rice

Rice, or *khao*, is not only a staple food in the Thai diet but also one of the country's major export commodities. In Thailand the cultivation and harvesting of rice is connected with life itself. Little wonder, then, that many Thai proverbs mention rice. The proverb *Khun khao daeng kaeng ron* literally means that one is indebted to the person who gives one shelter or food and obliged to show gratitude. The phrase *khao mai pla man* refers to newlyweds. The proverb *Chai khao plueak ying khao san* compares men and women to rice seeds and milled rice respectively. The rice seed will grow wherever it falls, whereas milled rice cannot grow. The proverb implies that in a relationship, the woman is replaceable; a man can always find a new partner.

Everyday Proverbs

Ram mai di, thot pi thot klong—"When you don't dance well, you blame it on the flute and the drum." This proverb chastises the bad dancer who would rather blame the orchestra than admit his or her lack of skill.

Chua chet thi, di chet hon—"Bad seven times, good seven times." Every cloud has a silver lining. Even if life treats one poorly and unfairly many times, one will eventually get a respite; one should persevere through difficult times because good times are likely "right around the corner".

Ya chap pla song mu—"Do not catch fish with both hands." This proverb is a warning against greed. One should take only what is needed, leaving some for other people.

Chaang phuak koet nai pa—"A white elephant is born in the wild." This saying attributes our good and bad qualities to nature rather than nurture; these qualities are innate.

Tham di dai di / Tham chua dai chua—"Good deeds beget good results, while bad deeds beget bad results."

Dai yang sia yang—"To obtain something, one must sacrifice something else."

Phakchi roi na—"To sprinkle parsley on the surface". This means to mislead or deceive someone.

Yom maew khai—"Dyeing the cat to sell it"

Sai takra lang nam—"To put oneself in the basket to wash oneself"

These two sayings mean that the true nature of something will always prevail, regardless of attempts to disguise it.

Buddhist Sayings and Quotations

Because Buddhism is an important influence in Thai life, many Thai people regard the sayings of the Buddha as wisdom.

"Do not speak—unless it improves on silence." Empty or frivolous speech destroys the beauty of that rare commodity, silence.

"You can explore the universe looking for somebody who is more deserving of your love and affection than you are yourself, and you will not find that person anywhere." "Your worst enemy cannot harm you as much as your own unguarded thoughts." These two sayings reveal the Buddhist emphasis on valuing and knowing oneself.

"Thousands of candles can be lit from a single candle, and the life of the candle will not be shortened."—from *Sutta Nipata*, part of the Buddhist scriptures. Happiness is not to be hoarded selfishly; it does not diminish or lose its value and impact when shared.

FOLKLORE

Folktales are passed down through the generations, imparting morals, values, information and historical lessons. Thai folklore often gives reasons for natural occurrences or explains the origins of natural landforms or phenomena. Variations of many Thai folktales are also told in neighbouring countries such as India, Malaysia and China—perhaps even as far away as in Europe or North America.

Legends

Legend has it that one of Lord Buddha's disciples, Phra Sangkachai, was very handsome. Many female worshippers fell in love with him, and the disciple was so upset that he prayed to be made ugly. His wish was granted, and today, in certain monasteries there are statues of a fat monk with crude features—Phra Sangkachai. Buddhist monks are not supposed to seek attention or admiration; even today, monks may hide their faces using their fans when presiding at ceremonies or offering a sermon.

Stories

A *pour quoi* story is a tale that explains why or how something happened. A folk tale is a story with a moral. These are examples of popular Thai stories:

Pour Quoi Story: The Bay of Siam

Long ago in the country of Siam, there was a man named Khun Keha, the kindest and most creative kite-maker in the kingdom. In his house was a small workshop where he taught children how to make their very own kite creation—to fashion the basic frame and cover it with handmade paper. Khun Keha would then help the children paint beautiful pictures on their kites.

Although he was now an old man, the kite-maker had built something quite amazing—a kite that was larger than a house. It was in fact the largest kite in the world. To build the kite, he had had to remove the end, ceiling and sides of his house. Of course now he no longer had a house, but he did have the biggest kite in all of Siam. This was no ordinary kite, and it required the strongest of winds in order for it to fly. Khun Keha had painted intricate designs on his kite, and he prayed to the gods that strong winds would blow so that all the children in the village could enjoy the kite.

In the Year of the Horse, on the first day of the waning moon, the winds came in strong from the ocean and swept over the forests, robust, strapping and continuous. Khun Keha was excited. He called all the children to his house to help fly the enormous kite.

There was magic in this giant kite—not only could it fly, the children and Khun Keha could also ride in it. They could hear the magic of birds' whistles as they flew past them, and could reach out and touch the clouds. The children and Khun Keha returned exhilarated from their flight.

One day when the giant kite was anchored at the kite-maker's house, there was the strongest wind. The kite moved back and forth so forcefully that Khun Keha thought the strings would break. Khun Keha tried to take the kite down and put it away but it was not possible, and his only option was to let the kite fly away. Khun Keha and the children never saw their kite again. But the people of southern Siam say that once upon a time, a giant kite bigger than a house fell to earth and ripped the earth open where it landed. And that is how the Bay of Siam was formed.

Folk Tale: There Really Are No Secrets

Long ago in Thailand, there was a king. His country was peaceful, the rice fields produced abundant harvests, and the royal Brahmin astrologer predicted peace and prosperity for many years to come. To add to the good fortune, a white elephant had been found at the start of the king's reign, so this was very fortuitous for everyone in the kingdom. By all counts, the king should have been very happy, but he was not. His face wore a dreariness and sadness that no one could explain.

Only one person in the entire kingdom—not the kings many royal wives, not his children—knew what was troubling the king. And that was the royal barber. He was sworn to secrecy. But one day the king's barber became gravely ill, and the job of cutting His Majesty's hair had to fall to a new barber.

The king revealed his important secret to the new barber, who was also sworn to secrecy. But there was a problem—the substitute barber simply could not keep a secret.

He finished the king's haircut and hurried home, but all the while the secret seethed inside him like a boiling volcano, waiting to explode. After a few days, the barber could bear it no more. He rowed to the middle of a river to shout out the secret, but there were fishermen everywhere. He went to the *wat*, but it was filled with worshippers. Frantic, he ran to the deepest part of the royal forest, where the trees were dense and majestic.

There was not a soul anywhere in any direction as far as the eye could see. Spying a huge tree with a hollow deep enough for a man to fit inside, he squeezed himself as far into the tree as possible, took the deepest of breaths and shouted into the inner trunk of the tree the secret that the king had told him. His voice echoed endlessly within the tree, but outside not a sound broke the silence of the forest. Relieved, the barber went home completely at peace.

Not long after the barber had told his secret, the Royal Orchestra became in need of a new drum. The royal drum-makers went deep into the forest to find the perfect tree to make the drum. And they chose the exact hollow tree to which the barber had told the king's secret. They chopped down the tree and it was fashioned into the most beautiful drum the kingdom had ever had.

People came from far and wide to see and hear the new drum. As crowds stood in the palace courtyard and the king waited on his terrace to hear the drum's first sounds, the drum spoke in the clearest and loudest human voice, "The king has moles on his head. The king has moles on his head." Every time the mallet touched the drum it boomed, "The king has moles on his head."

Now the entire kingdom knew why the king had been so unhappy. Furious, the king summoned the substitute barber to him. The barber admitted that he had spoken the secret to the tree when not one person was around. The wise king nodded and said, "The truth is what should always be told." He had the barber released and, turning to his people, declared, "There is no reason to hide one's faults or flaws. No one is perfect, and there is no such thing as a secret."

The king smiled then, and so did everyone who was watching. It was clear that the weight of sadness was gone from his person. The kingdom celebrated to the beat of the drum, which continued to boom, "The king has moles on his head. The king has moles on his head."

Myths

The story of Manora the Bird Woman is a very popular Thai myth that is told orally as well as in classical dance and drama. There are many similarities between this tale and an ancient Indian tale about a bird woman. The story is also told in Malaysia and performed in classical dance in Indonesia.

Manora and Prince Suthon

Once upon a time in Panchala Nakhon in the country of Siam, there was a kind, handsome and intelligent young prince named Prince Suthon. The prince was skilful at many things, but he was an extraordinary archer, earning him the nickname "Good Arrow". His parents the king and queen were very proud of him.

It came time for the prince to marry, and the king and queen searched for a perfect wife for him—someone not only beautiful but also kind, gracious and dignified. But there was something wrong with every young woman who wanted to be the prince's bride. One was not very clever, another's face turned pink every time someone talked to her, another didn't stand up straight, the fourth was very ugly, the fifth could not dance, the sixth couldn't sing, the seventh spoke too loudly and the eighth too softly. The king and queen were concerned and the entire kingdom was worried.

Now the palace had a famous royal hunter by the name of Pun. One day as he was out hunting he came across the secret bathing pool used by the seven beautiful daughters of King Tumerat, the king of the Bird People in a faraway kingdom to the north. The girls were considered the most beautiful in the world. They had soft, feathery, glistening wings that could be removed, and without them the girls looked like any other beautiful princesses.

When Pun saw the wings lying on the ground, he captured Manora, the most beautiful girl of all, and carried her back to the palace. The king and queen were enchanted with Manora. She was indeed the perfect wife for their son. Prince Suthon and Manora fell deeply in love and were married.

In time, the prince had to fight in a war and was forced to leave his wife behind. He asked a good friend to take care of Manora, making him the new royal court counsellor. The old royal court counsellor became jealous and plotted to save his position.

The night the prince left for battle, the king had a horrible dream that his kingdom was in danger. Seizing this opportunity to secure his position, the old royal court counsellor tricked the king into agreeing to sacrifice Manora to appease the gods and save his kingdom. The queen, however, helped Manora escape by bringing her her wings.

Manora flew to the home of a wise hermit who lived near the bathing pool where Pun had found her. She told him what had happened and gave him her red ruby ring, begging him to protect Prince Suthon and to give him the ring. The hermit promised to help the prince find Manora, and with that Manora flew home to her father and six sisters.

When the prince returned from battle and learned what had happened, he immediately set out to find Manora. He travelled days and weeks until he came across the same bathing pool where Pun had originally found Manora. There the hermit gave him Manora's ruby ring and did three things to help him on the dangerous journey to the Land of the Bird People: he gave him his monkey for protection, taught him special prayers and instructed him in the language of the birds and animals.

The prince travelled for seven years and seven months, through jungles, forests, fields and over high mountains. He survived many perilous obstacles using the skills the hermit had taught him. Finally he found the Land of the Bird People and was reunited with Manora.

But the king made him perform three difficult tasks to test his worthiness: to lift a stone bench in the royal garden; to identify Manora from seven identical maidens; and to shoot a single arrow through seven palm boards, seven fig wood boards, seven plates of copper, seven plates of iron and seven bullock carts of sand. Prince Suthon completed the first two tasks by praying to the gods and did not hesitate with the third. True to his nickname "Good Arrow", he pierced the seven palm boards, seven fig wood boards, seven plates of copper, seven plates of iron and seven bullock carts of sand with a single swift arrow.

And from that moment on, with the king's blessing, Prince Suthon and Manora lived happily ever after, producing many children and grandchildren who all lived happily ever after in the kingdom of Panchala Nakhon.

MYTHICAL CREATURES

Singhas (lions originating in Burmese folklore) are symbols of strength and power. Usually portrayed open-mouthed consuming their prey, they are often positioned outside the temple doors. Above a temple window or door may be the monster called *kala*, the Hindu god of time and death, usually portrayed as a disembodied head with bulging eyes and sharp upper teeth. Popular in Chiang Mai temples is the *kinnari*, a creature with the head, torso and arms of a beautiful woman and the wings, tail and legs of a swan. The *kinnari* is a traditional symbol of feminine beauty and grace. Also common in northern Thailand is the *hongse*, a mythical swan-like creature on which rode Brahma, the Hindu god of creation. *Hongse* are often perched atop high poles adorning gates.

PERFORMING ARTS

Because many historical records were lost when Ayutthaya fell to Burma in 1767, relatively little is known about the Thai arts prior to the classical or Bangkok period beginning in 1782. We do know, however, that traditional Thai musical instruments evolved from ancient Indian and Chinese instruments. Thai classical dance traces its roots to 1431, when the Tai peoples captured Angkor and kidnapped the royal Khmer dance troupe. Because all other records were lost in 1767, however, we do not know which dance forms existed before 1431.

King Ramkhamhaeng mentioned instruments such as the *phin, sang, pichanai, krajappi, chakhe* and *thon* in the Tribhumikatha, one of the first written Thai books, and on an inscription from the Sukhothai period. Four to eight musicians made up the musical ensembles during the Ayutthaya period, and vocal music was composed in suites called *phleng rua*. Most lyrics were adapted from the *Ramakien.*

In the classical or Bangkok period, beginning in 1782, the Thai arts experienced a renaissance that produced some beautiful music and lyrics. Today, the Music Association of Thailand is supported by royal patronage. There has been an increase in government and royal sponsorship of Thai classical music since the mid-20th century.

TRADITIONAL MUSIC

There are three types of orchestras in Thailand: *pi phat*, the classical music ensemble that performs for the court and at the theatre; *khryang sai*, which is a village ensemble; and *mahori*, the classical ensemble that accompanies vocalists.

The *pi phat* is dominated by percussion instruments and flutes. It traditionally includes an oboe (*pi nai*), two xylophones (*ranat*), barrel drums (*klong*) and two sets of tuned gong-chimes (*kong wong*) but different combinations of instruments make up the various *pi phat* ensembles that accompany specific kinds of performances, such as shadow puppet theatre, *khon* classical theatre or the *likay* performance.

The *khryang sai* is primarily a string ensemble typically consisting of the *solaw* (a bowed lute), *jakhae* (a three-stringed plucked instrument resembling a zither), several *khlui* (flutes) of different sizes, a drum and sometimes a *khim* (Chinese dulcimer). The *khryang sai* often accompanies a stick puppet theatre performance. The ensemble has a distinctive Chinese sound, reflecting its probable Chinese origins.

The *mahori* is a classical music ensemble played by court women in central Thailand. Originally musicians played smaller instruments (in keeping with their size), but today, regular sized instruments are used—with a combination of instruments from both the *khryang sai* and the *pi phat*.

Some Popular Thai Musical Instruments

Khryang ditt are stringed instruments played by plucking. The *jakhae*, believed to have developed from the earlier *phin* instrument, is a three-stringed, eleven-fretted instrument with a hollow body. It is held horizontally and played with the musician seated on the ground. Originally, the instrument was shaped like a crocodile, with the front carved to look like jaws. The Thai word for crocodile is *ja ra kay*, which became shortened to *jakhae* for the instrument. Today, the *jakhae* is loved for its beautiful, resonant tone and is an important member of all string ensembles. The *krajappi* is a four-stringed instrument representing a lute. Its name is derived from the ancient Pali-Sanskrit word *gatchapa*, meaning "turtle". The resonance chamber of the *krajappi* looks a bit like the shell of a turtle.

Khryang sii are stringed instruments played with a bow. The *saw sam sai* is a three-stringed instrument with a sound chamber made from half a coconut shell and covered with either goat or calfskin. The *saw u* is two-stringed and fretless, with an oval-shaped coconut-shell sound chamber. The *saw duang* is a two-stringed instrument with a cylindrical sound chamber. It could have been named for its resemblance to a type of lizard (*duang dak yae*) trap found in northern Thailand.

Khryang tii are percussion instruments. These may be made of wood, metal or leather. The *ranad ek* and r*anad thum* are two Thai percussive instruments made of wood. A string is threaded through several wooden rectangles or keys that produce different tones when struck. Two wooden knob-ended sticks are used to play the instrument. The *ranad thum* evolved from the *ranad ek*, with longer and wider keys and a different shape.

Metal percussion instruments include several types of cymbals and gongs. Gongs are used for religious ceremonies, but also very important in Thai traditional musical ensembles. The *khawng wong yai* and *khawng wong lek* are, respectively, large and small tuned gongs struck by a knobbed hammer. The player sits in the middle of the circle of gongs.

Ching and *chab* are types of cymbals played by hitting a pair together. One type is shaped like a cup and the other like a small hollow cone. The cymbal pairs are held together by a short cord.

Percussion instruments made of leather include an array of *glawng* (drums). Thai drums are played with the palm and fingers. The *thone mahori* drum is a vase-shaped vessel made of pottery or ceramic. The head, or large sound chamber, is covered with calf, goat or sometimes snakeskin. The drummer controls the tone of the drum by closing or opening the mouth, or small end of the instrument, with his hand. The *thone mahori* is played together with the *ram mana*, a drum resembling a large tambourine without metal discs.

Khryang paw are wind instruments. *Khlui* are wooden flutes played vertically like the clarinet or oboe. They come in different lengths, each with a different tonal range. The *pi* is a wind instrument with a reed. It often accompanies shadow puppet theatre. It is made of hardwood or marble. The *pi cha nai* is a two-part wind instrument with a reed; the top is cylindrical and the bottom is bell-shaped. The instrument is made of wood or ivory and is used in royal funeral and military processions.

Famous Thai Musicians

Phra Chen Duriyang (Peter Feit) was an accomplished musician who had studied the piano and stringed instruments. He founded Thailand's first orchestra in the Royal Entertainment Department. He also composed the Thai national anthem in 1932, when he was the royal music advisor to the Thai court.

Montri Tramote and Khunying Phaitoon Kittivan are two well-known Thai musicians. They were conferred National Artist status in 1985 and 1986 respectively for their contribution to Thai music. Montri Tramote was an accomplished musician, author, composer and guest lecturer. His knowledge of Western music enriched and enhanced his work in Thai music. Khunying Phaitoon Kittivan played an integral role in the revival of Thai classical music. A renowned speaker and expert on Thai ancient vocal music, she taught music both at institutions and to the Thai princesses Maha Chakri Sirindhorn and Chulabhorn.

King Bhumibol Adulyadej, an internationally recognised jazz musician, has composed several music pieces, including one featured in a Broadway show in the 1950s. In 1964 Vienna's NQ Tonkunstler Orchestra played a selection of the King's compositions at the Vienna Concert Hall in Austria.

Princess Maha Chakri Sirindhorn is an accomplished musician on several Thai classical instruments. She has been very active in renewing interest in Thai classical music among the people in Thailand.

DANCE

Classical Thai Dance

Classical Thai dance is truly an art form unlike any other in the world, with virtually no Western influence. Thai dance is made up of hundreds of *ma boad* (mother verses), each a mini-dance or pose, that when combined form a story in dance. A student must learn and perfect all the steps to be able to interpret music and story into dance. Thai dance originated as an offering to the gods, performed only within the royal palace for a heavenly rather than an earthly audience. As time passed, Thai dance became popular and was permitted outside the royal palace.

Dancers maintain a straight back and "centre" while dancing; the swaying and leaning movements come from different feet positions. The hands are the dancer's key instruments and the focus of much training and exercise. The hand movements of Thai classical dance demand great gracefulness and dexterity.

Folk Dance

The northern, northeastern and southern parts of Thailand all have traditional folk dances unique to each region. The graceful and gentle folk dances of northern Thailand, *fon*, are performed by women. The *fon lep*, or fingernail dance, is a favourite. This dance is usually performed to welcome important visitors or royal guests. The traditional costume is a tube skirt, blouse and shawl. The dancer wears her hair in a bun, to which an orchid or flowers are attached. In the *fon thian*, or candle dance, each dancer holds a lit candle. The dance is graceful and beautiful, especially under the night sky.

Dancers of northeastern Thailand perform *soeng*, which are similar to *fon* but with faster movements. *Soeng* are often performed during the Candle Festival of Buddhist Lent. Another type of folk show that combines narrative, singing and live music is the *mo lam*.

The *nora,* an art form combining dance and drama, is unique to southern Thailand. Hand movements are an integral part of the dance routine. The most popular is the folk story of Prince Suthon and Manora the Bird Woman (see *Proverbs and Folklore*). Singers wear beautifully coloured costumes with white socks and finger extenders.

NINE-INCH FINGER EXTENDERS

In many traditional folk dances, the dancers wear silver finger extenders on all fingers excluding the thumbs. The extenders accentuate the importance of the movements and gestures, bringing attention to the shape and curve of the dancer's fingers. There are even special extenders for different regional dances. Originally, nail extenders were made from precious metals such as gold and silver. Most today are made from stainless steel and are more affordable. A set of extenders consists of eight 'nails' and is sized to the age of the dancer. The 'nails' are attached by tape after the dancer is fully dressed.

DRAMA

The *khon* form of drama developed from Indian temple rituals, with storylines from the Indian classic the *Ramayana*. In Thailand, the drama evolved into a formal, masked performance of the *Ramakien* that combines dance, drama, singing, acrobatics and music. Originally performed for the Thai royal court at special occasions such as births, marriages and funerals, *khon* drama boasts elaborate costumes and movements that are very formalised and rhythmic. Every movement has a meaning. A Thai traditional *pi phat* orchestra offstage accompanies the performance. The music helps create the mood of the performance.

The *lakhon* dramatic form is very similar to the *khon* but less formal. Actors portraying human and celestial characters do not wear masks, and folktales and scenes from the *Ramakien* may be performed.

The *likay* is thought to have originated from Muslim religious performances and is usually performed by travelling groups for local audiences. A very informal type of drama, it may combine comedy, melodrama, folklore and dance. A *pi phat* orchestra accompanies the performance. There may be slapstick comedy routines and social satire. The actors interact with the audience, and there are lots of jokes and improvisational routines, some of which can be quite risqué. Performances are held indoors during the rainy season and usually outdoors during the dry season. The *manohra* is southern Thailand's counterpart to the *likay*. It is based primarily on scenes from the *Ramakien* and includes both dance and drama.

Puppet Theatre

In Thai shadow puppet theatre, puppets and puppeteers are positioned behind a backlit screen elevated about 2 m above the ground. The audience sits in a dark setting, such as in a darkened theatre or outdoors at night. This type of theatre is closely related to the Indonesian *wayang* puppet theatre. There are two types of shadow puppets: *nang yai* and *nang talung*. Both are made from cow or buffalo leather intricately carved and perforated into silhouettes of humans, animals, gods, mythical creatures and other 'actors' in the play. The figures are placed on sticks. Measuring about 2 m high and 1 m wide, *nang yai* puppets are controlled by puppeteers who move along with their puppets for the entire duration of the show. *Nang* yai performances are rare nowadays. More common *nang talung* performances feature much smaller puppets with several moveable body parts that the puppeteer can manipulate sitting down. The storylines are often drawn from folklore, and the dialogue between characters is informal, humorous and lively.

Hand puppets called *hun krabok* are similar to Punch and Judy hand puppets. The head is first carved from wood, then lacquered and painted. A bamboo rod is attached to the neck, and the puppet is given a costume like those in Thai classical dance. The plot typically consists of stories from the *Ramakien*. Thai artist and puppet-maker Chakrabhand Posayakrit, who works with both *hun* and *nang yai* puppets, has revitalised rod puppet theatre in Thailand.

Film and Television

Most Thai films are produced solely for entertainment and include popular actors with wide appeal. One actor may play many roles in different films being produced simultaneously. Some of the most admired filmmakers include Prince Panupan Yukgla, Dokdin, Kanyamal, Piak Poster and Cherd

Songsri. For the most part, films are produced for profit, although a handful of filmmakers include social commentary. Filmmaker Wichit Khunawut has directed serious films such as *Khon Phu Khao* (*Mountain People*), which deals with the northern hill tribes; and *Luk Isan* (*Son of the Northeast*), which focusses on poverty and hardship in northeastern Thailand.

Foreign-made films with scenes filmed in Thailand include *The Killing Fields* (1984), *Tomorrow Never Dies* (1997), *The Beach* (2000), *Around the World in 80 Days* (2004), *Bridget Jones: The Edge of Reason* (2004), *Star Wars: Episode III Revenge of the Sith* (2005), *Stealth* (2005) and *American Gangster* (2007).

Thai television features both local and cable viewing possibilities in a variety of languages. American television series and movies; reality television shows; local MTV; international sports coverage; Japanese cartoons; and Chinese and Thai dramas and soap operas are the Thai people's most popular choices.

ARTS AND
ARCHITECTURE

PAINTING

Prehistoric Painting

Archaeologists have discovered prehistoric paintings on the two sheer cliffs overlooking the Mekong River in Pha Taem National Park in Ubon Ratchathani. These paintings date back 3,000–4,000 years and include geometric patterns, hand prints and figures of animals and people hunting and fishing—reflections of life in this region in prehistoric times. The Pha Taem is the largest prehistoric rock-painting site in Thailand. There are four groups of red-ochre paintings, with a total of more than 300 images.

Thai Painting

Relatively little is known about Thai painting prior to 1767, because much Ayutthaya artwork was destroyed when the kingdom fell to the Burmese. Classical Thai paintings survive in book illustrations, on murals and in palace and temple interiors in Thailand. Figures were two-dimensional, without shadowing or perspective and were sized to reflect their status in relation to one another. Separate vignettes were painted within the same picture or mural, so that several scenes seem to occupy the same 'space' or canvas, or several events appear to be taking place at the same time in isolation from the others. In fact these scenes are all part of the entire painting, almost like depicting each activity in each room in the cross-section of a house, for instance.

The traditional pigments used were close to scarlet, yellow ochre, ultramarine blue, white and pot-black, and the artist mixed these basic colours to create his palette. The medium was tempera powders combined with a binding agent, usually a glue of sorts. Sticks or pieces of wood were used to mix the colours. Temple murals on walls, banners on cloth and illustrated manuscripts on handcrafted paper were created with these paints.

The earliest murals in Thailand, such as those of Wat Suthat in Bangkok and Wat Suwannaram in Thon Buri, were created with natural pigments and depict the *Jataka Tales*, a collection of folklore-like literature describing the previous births and lives of Lord Buddha.

MURAL PAINTINGS

Within the Temple of the Emerald Buddha are 178 panels of murals depicting the *Ramakien* tales. In 1807, King Rama I had written the *Ramakien*, the Thai version of the Indian *Ramayana* epic. The original painting dates from the reign of King Rama III (1824–1851) but the murals have been restored and repainted on numerous occasions, most recently in 1982 in celebration of Bangkok's 200th anniversary.

From the late 18th century onwards, during the Classical or Bangkok period, colours became more intense because imported pigments from China became available. In the mid-19th century, chemical pigments reached Thailand and painters began incorporating the Western technique of perspective into artwork. In contrast with the natural pigments used in earlier murals, later paintings employed strong and vibrant primary colours and gold leaf (gold in the form of very thin foil, as for gilding). Thai murals during this period depicted Lord Buddha with golden skin and wearing red robes—a fusion of myth and reality, with Buddhist and Hindu traditions well represented.

As Thai painters experimented increasingly with Western styles and techniques, they produced many unique works of art. Two artists who have blended traditional Thai with Western art are Thawan Dachanee and Chakrapan Posayakrit. Educated in Bangkok and Amsterdam, Thawan's oil paintings and ink illustrations are exhibited in public galleries and prized by private art collectors. Chakrapan Posayakrit is best known for his portraits and his scenes of Thai literature, in which traditional motifs, themes and scenes are given a modern treatment.

SCULPTURE

The Mon Dvaravati and Haripunjaya Period

Art of this period (from the 7th to 11th century) was dominated by religious sculpture. In the Dvaravati kingdom, subjects from Buddhism and Hinduism were cast in stone, stucco, terracotta and bronze. Although this style of art was strongly influenced by the Amaravati (southern India), Gupta and Post-Gupta art types from the 4th to 8th century, such details as the facial features of the sculptures were noticeably Southeast Asian.

Sculpted in the round, the Wheel of Law was a very important subject of ancient Indian art, with many uncovered in the Dvaravati kingdom from the 7th century. Thought to depict Lord Buddha's first sermon in the deer park at Sarnath near Benares, the wheel features many carved images of deer figures. It is sometimes decorated with floral motifs and images of flames. The National Museum in Bangkok houses many examples of this type of sculpture.

Sculptures from the Mon kingdom of Haripunjaya (Lamphun today) were distinctive for the absence of Hindu subjects. Primarily Buddhist subjects in 9th- to 10th-century Indian dress were cast in stone, terracotta, stucco and bronze. Facial features were Indian-influenced—very stylised, with curly hair, well-proportioned bodies, prominent eyes, incised moustaches and neck wrinkles). Good examples of this art can be seen in Lamphun at the National Museum, Wat Phra That Haripunjaya and Wat Chamatewi.

During the Dvaravati period, depictions of Lord Buddha became standardised to represent spiritual purity and inner peace. Some 30 stylised features, including fingers and toes of even length, 40 evenly spaced and gapless teeth, a white wisp of hair in the centre of the brow and smooth skin, distinguished images of the Buddha from representations of humans or of other deities. The Hindu gods, for instance, were depicted very differently, as superhumans of kingly stature with beautiful faces, crowned and ornamented with jewels. Good displays of Dvaravati art can be viewed at the National Museum in U Tong and the Jim Thompson Museum and National Museum in Bangkok.

Srivijaya Art

Srivijaya Art of southern Thailand is a blend of art styles from Champa (Vietnam), Central Java and India from the 7th to 11th century. During this period, the Sailendra Dynasty of Central Java ruled the Malay Peninsula and southern Thailand to the Isthmus of Kra—the narrow neck of southern Burma and Thailand that joins the Malay Peninsula to the Asian Mainland, lying between the Gulf of Thailand to the east and the Andaman Sea to the west.

Srivijaya sculpture reflected the Mahayana Buddhism that was predominant in this region. Sculptures include Buddha images and ornamental pillars. The Srivijaya capital was Grahi (now Chaiya in the province of Surat Thani), once a thriving trade centre located just south of the Isthmus of Kra. A good selection of Srivijaya art bronzes are on display at the National Museums in Bangkok and Nakhon Si Thammarat and the Museum at Wat Phra Mahathat in Chaiya.

Lop Buri Art

Lop Buri sculpture from the 11th to 13th century in the central valley was predominantly Buddhist. Some of the best examples are the 12th-century Crowned Buddha from Ayutthaya and the Bodhisattva Head from Nakhon Ratchasima. Other works are displayed at the National Museum in Bangkok and at regional museums.

The Sukhothai Era

Theravada Buddhism had a profound influence on Sukhothai sculpture during the 14th and 15th centuries. Buddhist art reached its height during this period, and many Buddha images, reflecting compassion and divinity, were created in bronze, stucco and stone. The finest examples include the 'walking' Buddha at Wat Phra Ratana Mahathat, the stucco Buddhas at Wat Mahathat Sukhothai and Wat Si Chun, the National Museum in Bangkok and the Ramkhamhaeng Museum in Sukhothai Historical Park.

The Ayutthaya Period

Early art from the Ayutthaya Kingdom reveals both Dvaravati and Lop Buri influences. Later, from the 15th century onwards, Ayutthaya developed its own artistic style, primarily influenced by Sukhothai and U Thong. Khmer influences are apparent from the 17th century onwards, when Ayutthaya expanded into Khmer lands. From the late17th century until about 1767, Buddha images excessively decorated with crowns and robes were popular. Ayutthaya sculpture was produced in bronze, wood, stucco and sandstone, but much of the art was destroyed during the Burmese invasions.

The Rattanakosin Period

From the time of the collapse of Ayutthaya in 1767 to the beginning of the Chakri Dynasty in Bangkok, there was strong support and endorsement for classical Siamese artistic traditions. Efforts were made to move artworks, including sculptures, from war-torn regions to Bangkok to preserve an archive for the country.

In the 18th and 19th centuries, Thai artists absorbed Western and modern techniques. Images became more lifelike. The form of the human body in painting and sculpture, including hairstyles and clothing, became more true-to-form.

THE MANY FACES OF THE BUDDHA

With approximately 30,000 monasteries in the country, each possessing a central image of the Buddha, Buddha sculptures and statues are ubiquitous in Thailand. Each image is considered a surrogate for the Lord Buddha, with a life of its own. Most homes even have an altar or a separate room with a principal Buddha image and possibly also smaller ones. Images range in size from 1 cm (such as on an amulet one would carry on one's person) to the 14.7-m seated statue of Buddha Phra Achana at Wat Si Chum in Sukhothai. People honour the Buddha statue by touching their forehead to the ground three times—once for the Buddha, once for the Buddhist doctrine and once for the monkhood. This is called the Triple Gem.

Bronze casting has been the predominant sculpture medium since the 14th century, but Buddhas have been produced in a variety of media. During the 19th century, the Russian goldsmith and jeweller Fabergé accepted commissions from the Thai court to produce a Buddha in jade and rubies.

THE EMERALD BUDDHA

The Emerald Buddha is reputedly the most sacred statue in Thailand. Measuring about 66 cm in height, the image is made of green jade. Its exact origin is unknown, but experts conclude that it was probably made in northern Thailand or southern India. Legend has it that in 1434, lightning struck a temple in Chiang Rai and a Buddha image was discovered within, completely encased in stucco. After the abbot noticed that the stucco was peeling and had it removed, the beautiful Emerald Buddha was revealed. The statue was moved to Chiang Mai, taken to Laos in 1551, then returned to Thailand in 1778. When Bangkok became the capital of Thailand, the Emerald Buddha was placed in the Temple of the Emerald Buddha at Wat Phra Kaew in 1784. King Rama I had two robes made for the Emerald Buddha—one for summer and another for the rainy season; King Rama III added a third robe for winter. King Bhumibol Adulyadej ceremonially changes the robes himself each season.

ARCHITECTURE

Srivijaya Architecture

Buildings of the Srivijaya kingdom consist mainly of Mahayana Buddhist structures. Examples such as the Phra Borom Mathat (dating from the 9th to 10th century) and Wat Kaew Pagoda in Chaiya can be viewed along the eastern coastline, from the province of Surat Thani to the province of Songkhla.

The Sukhothai Era

Buildings constructed from wood during this era did not withstand the centuries, but ruins reveal the development of a distinctive architecture. Temples had open walls, columns of stone and a wooden roof with two slopes and a gable at each end. The strong influence of 9th- to 13th-century Khmer architecture is apparent in the layout of temple grounds, which conforms to the Hindu perspective of the nature of the universe.

The Ayutthaya Period

The prosperity of Siam during this time is reflected in its architecture—in the regal opulence of buildings fitted with golden spires. Thick walls, huge columns and narrow windows were characteristic of temple halls. The *chedi* (a Buddhist mound-like structure) and *prang* (a tall finger-like spire) of the memorial towers grew taller and narrower, with the *prang* becoming an integral component, as in Khmer architecture. From the 13th to 15th centuries, Chinese techniques such as lacquer painting and ceramic tiling were employed for roofs and ornamentation. As Western influence strengthened from the mid-16th century, Thai designs incorporated some Western motifs, such as the leaves of the acanthus (a shrub indigenous to the Mediterranean). During the reign of King Narai in the 17th century, foreign influence was extensive. Some of this is reflected in the palaces and forts built in Ayutthaya, Lopburi and Bangkok at this time.

The Rattanakosin Period

During the reign of Rama I, a central focus of art was to raise morale and renew infrastructure. In architecture, attempts were made to recapture the splendour of Ayutthaya. As Western influence grew stronger, Western architectural styles influenced Thai construction. The Chakri Mahaprasad Hall of the Grand Palace in Bangkok, for instance, was designed by British architects and built in 1882 by Thai labour. Its style is influenced by the Italian Renaissance. By the mid-19th century, architecture had become more colourful, utilising a fusion of different styles. Increasing commerce between Thailand and China led to pervasive Chinese influence in architectural detailing, for instance in ceramic roof tiling and coloured glazing. Chinese stone statues were imported and placed in both palace and temple courtyards.

THE GRAND PALACE

Until the end of the absolute monarchy in 1932, the Grand Palace was the king's main residence, the centre of royal services and the headquarters for government. In the early 20th century, Rama V moved to the current royal residence, Dusit Palace. However the Grand Palace remains the centre for royal and official ceremony.

Built by Rama I, the Grand Palace was intended not only to celebrate and announce the beginning of the Chakri Dynasty but also to serve as a prototype of the Grand Palace of Ayutthaya. Most of the architecture was constructed during the first four reigns of the Chakri Dynasty and combines Thai, Chinese and Western influences, styles and materials. Covering an approximate area of 2.4 sq km, the Grand Palace is enclosed by fortified walls crowned with six octagonal and three square towers. The Central Court includes the royal residences and the spired throne halls, where ceremonies take place. The Inner Court was for the king and royal family only, and even though it is no longer the royal residence, it remains entirely closed to the public. The Outer Court is for offices, including the royal treasury and some military and civilian ministries and bureaus.

THAI RELIGIOUS ARCHITECTURE

Temples

Up to the Ayutthaya period in Siam, only temples could be built with permanent materials such as stone, brick and stucco, because they were regarded as the most important buildings in the land. Palaces and other buildings were made of less durable materials, such as wood. Buddhist kings earned merit and also displayed the power of their kingdoms by building temples.

A traditional structure on *wat* compounds is the drum or bell tower, originally built so that a drum (*ho klong*) or bell (*ho rakhang*) could be struck to announce time, religious services and other important events. The tower is typically square, with a special roof topped with spires or gables resembling the ones on royal pavilions.

The northern kingdom of Lan Na endured from the 13th to 18th centuries and did not become part of Siam until the 19th century. In this part of the country, temples were built mainly of wood. Roofs are large and low, and the compound includes open pavilions called *viharn*. Burmese influence is evident in the building of multi-tiered (three, five, seven or nine tiers) roofs.

In northeastern Thailand the typical *wat* is simple, with roofs extending upwards rather than outwards like those in northern Thailand. The open or partially enclosed ordination hall is small and built of wood or plastered brick.

A *wat* in southern Thailand may combine a variety of characteristics and influences including Chinese decorations and motifs. The paintings and roofs of monks' quarters may reflect Malay and Sino-Portuguese influences.

Further details on the purpose and layout of Thai *wat* and the religious functions of its buildings are included in the *Religion* chapter.

THE TEMPLE OF THE EMERALD BUDDHA

Widely regarded as Thailand's most significant religious location, Wat Phra Kaew, or the Temple of the Emerald Buddha, adjoins the Grand Palace in Bangkok and consists of more than 100 brightly coloured buildings. Around its perimeter are eight *prang* covered in different coloured mosaics. Also in the compound are two golden *chedi*. It is claimed that the ashes of the Buddha are interred in the Phra Si Rattana Chedi. Statues representing the 12 guardian giants from the *Ramakien* are positioned at the cloister entrances surrounding the temple. There are no monks' quarters as monks do not reside at the royal temple.

Mosques

Mosques number about 3,000 in Thailand, and their architecture is a fusion of local characteristics and Middle Eastern or Indian styles. Some mosques may even combine Rattanakosin, Western, Moorish and Southeast Asian features in their design.

NON-RELIGIOUS ARCHITECTURE

Traditional Houses

The gable roof is a distinctive design element of the traditional Thai house. Typically made of bamboo or wood, traditional houses were built on stilts, with a space beneath that served a variety of purposes. Houses were usually built close to water sources. Today many individuals and organisations are working to preserve existing examples of traditional Thai architecture.

Houses in central Thailand typically have steep-sloping roofs adapted to annual monsoon rains and tropical heat. Columns and walls angled inwards fortify the structure and increase the slope of the roof, so that water drains off better. The steep overhang of the roof also allows air currents to circulate and cool the house during the hottest times of the year.

In northern Thailand, the sloping roof beams extend beyond the ridgepole (the topmost, centre roof beam) to form a V-shape (*kalae*) at either end of the roof. The purpose of this unusual and distinctive design feature is unclear. Unlike the houses of central Thailand, the walls of the northern house lean slightly outwards. One of the most important aspects of the house is the porch or verandah (*toen*), a raised platform that served by day as a living area and by night as a sleeping place for the males of the family or for male guests.

Immigrants from Laos have influenced the architecture in northeastern Thailand, but houses are also similar to those in central Thailand. Because the climate is drier, however, the roofs are less sloped, and many are made from corrugated iron. Walls are vertical, leaning neither inwards nor outwards.

Traditional houses in southern Thailand may have features of Malay origin and design as well as bear the influence of colonial Dutch and/or English architecture, probably from Indonesia. Carved wooden detailing is distinctive, and fretted wood ornamentation is common.

Water is historically important to the Thai people, for sustenance as well as transportation. Some traditional houses are built directly on waterways, supported by tall posts over the water. This type of house, the *baan rim naam*, has a float made of bamboo or wood below the cabin of the house. This pontoon enables the house to move with the tide and even to float during floods.

CHINESE DESIGN IN ART AND ARCHITECTURE

Centuries of Chinese immigration have left their mark on many aspects of Thai culture and life, including architecture, design and decoration. Religious and royal architecture, lacquer painting decoration and motifs and some of the colour combinations that feature in Thai art and architecture are distinctively Chinese. Palace roofs often hint at Chinese influence, and the stone mountains and bonsai found in Thai gardens are Chinese-inspired. There are many Chinese images in Thai mural paintings, and the red and gold of temple interiors is certainly reminiscent of Chinese decoration.

COURTYARD GARDENS

Thai courtyard gardens combine European, Chinese and Japanese influences, eclectically drawing on the best of each. Traditional Thai gardens typically juxtapose garden structures such as terracotta planters, large rocks, stucco figures of mythical figures and creatures and miniature *chedi* against a natural backdrop of plants, shrubs and trees. Plants typical in both formal (temple and royal gardens) and home gardens include bonsai, brightly coloured flowers and fragrant trees and shrubs. They are often chosen because they can be used in merit-making, religious events or other ceremonies. Sometimes herbs are specifically planted for their medicinal or culinary value. Unlike Japanese and Chinese bonsai, Thai bonsai are cultivated and shaped in an art of tree bending and clipping called *mai dat*, somewhat similar to topiary. The branches and leaves are shaped to form small globes (often three, five, seven, nine or eleven— considered auspicious numbers in Thailand).

Thai gardens are supposed to be viewed in small sections, like scenes in a play, movements in a classical sonata or sections of a Thai mural. Each element in a section enhances the others, giving the section its own beauty, tempo, rhythm and meaning. Religious gardens frequently contain a *bodhi* tree, under which Lord Buddha reputedly sat when he attained enlightenment.

The garden at the Grand Palace in Bangkok features large Chinese-inspired stones in combination with quintessentially Thai *mai dat* and mythical Hindu statues.

HANDICRAFTS

From religious items like alms bowls to decorative ceramics and lacquerware, and from Thai silk to the colourful embroidered pieces of the hill tribes, the Thai people have good reason to be proud of the handicrafts and artifacts that have been made by Thai craftspeople for hundreds of years.

RELIGIOUS ARTICLES

Alms Bowls

In the early morning throughout neighbourhoods and villages in Thailand, monks silently walk through the streets with their alms bowls to collect their daily food. They stop at each house for a few minutes, and if no one appears, they move on. By providing food for the monks, the lay community is making merit and also supporting the local monastery.

In the time of Lord Buddha, alms bowls were made of clay and iron. The traditional alms bowl today is a simple, spherical, covered bowl made of stainless steel or iron, or occasionally of clay or lacquerware. There are three parts to an alms bowl—the stand, the bowl and the lid. A clay bowl is produced from two firings in a kiln, and an iron bowl from five, to prevent rust.

Lenten Candles

Before electricity was readily available, candles and lanterns were used for commonplace as well as ceremonial functions. Offerings to monks would consist of beeswax for making candles. During the Annual Rains Retreat, in particular, monks would remain within the local temple to spend long hours studying and candles would be needed for light.

Today, during the Annual Rains Retreat parade, lit candles are placed in floats for all to enjoy. Although most temples are supplied with electricity, people still present candles to temples as a form of merit-making.

Monks' Fans

During ceremonies, Buddhist monks carry decorated fans. In early times, fans were made from palm leaves with short handles. They were perhaps originally used to protect the monk from harsh, unpleasant smells or to cover the monk's face so that worshippers could focus on his sermons.

Today, the offering of monks' fans to the temple is a merit-making opportunity. The more beautiful the fan, the greater its merit-making value. The most elaborate fans are made of carved ivory or embellished with rich embroidered cloths of satin or silk and even gemstones.

Gold Leaf

Gold leaf is real gold in the form of very thin foil, as for gilding. It is made by stacking gold and pounding it into paper-thin sheets that are then cut into small pieces with a sharp blade.

At a Buddhist temple, worshippers make money offerings and pay their respects to the main Buddha image. They light candles and burn sticks of incense, then place pieces of gold leaf on the image.

Gold leaf is also used in decorating and as an art material—for gilding picture frames, statues, paper, art and other objects such as jewellery.

HANDICRAFTS

Masks

Masks are a distinctive and unique part of traditional Thai dramatic arts. In the past, masks were worn by all the characters except female humans, goddesses and some female demons. Today, only animal characters perform wearing masks.

Mask-making is an art that has been passed down from generation to generation. Traditionally a master would select a young apprentice artist with talent and the desire to learn. Today mask-making is becoming an endangered art. Several artists may participate in the different stages of making or repairing a single mask. Fifteen layers of papier mâché (made from delicate *koi* paper, the same type of paper on which Lord Buddha's writings are transcribed for temple manuscripts) are applied to a plaster mould. Once the glue has dried, the mould is removed and a resin called *lac,* from the sumac tree, is applied in strips to accent and build up the mouth, ears and eyebrows on the mask. Additional decorations may include gold leaf, imitation gemstones (for a tiara or crown) and the details painted on the mask itself.

A *khon* mask is a very revered object, and several rites and customs are observed regarding its completion and its use. Once the mask is finished, it must be blessed. Each mask must be given protection by the gods in a special ceremony, or it is believed that disaster may befall the wearer of the mask. Before the first performance involving the mask, the master or head teacher must recite special words and place gold leaf at the centre of the forehead on the mask before putting the mask on the actor-dancer. When not in use, the masks are stored in a high place as a mark of respect to the spirits of the masks.

OF DEMONS AND MONKEYS

There are more than 100 different kinds of demon masks, each distinguished by its own colour, facial appearance and type of crown. The characteristics of each demon are established by tradition and mask-makers must comply with these conventions. The main part of the demon mask may be red, white, blue or green, and the eyes, mouth and nose are of contrasting colours. Demon eyes may be bulging (open) or 'crocodile' (lidded and half-closed). Mouths may be scowling or shut tight, with teeth showing. Teeth can be curved like tusks or straight like fangs. The demon Tosakan has a green face, bulging eyes, a scowling mouth and curved tusk-like teeth. He wears a three-tiered crown.

There are 30–40 monkey masks, also distinguished by colour, facial expression and crown. Monkeys have bulging eyes with either open or closed mouths. Monkeys may be bald or wear a crown or headdress, depending on the character. The most important and powerful monkey is Hanuman. As Rama's entrusted general, Hanuman has a white mask with green and pink accents and a red and gold tiara. His mouth is open, and there is a sparkling jewel on the roof of his mouth. The jewel between Hanuman's eyebrows is a symbol of inner power.

Textiles

Textiles in Thailand are primarily made from silk, cotton and jute, the strong, coarse fibres of a plant in the linden family. Weaving is a well-known and traditionally women's handicraft. Historically, certain fabrics and textiles represented a certain status; the royal family and the Buddhist religious community had special fabrics. Woven fabrics are used for clothing and for purses and decorative items.

Most weaving today is done in northern and northeastern Thailand. Patterns, fabric and weaving techniques vary, from bold and colourful hill tribe textiles and cottons in northern Thailand to intricate *pha mudmee* patterns on silks and cottons in northeastern Thailand. *pha mudmee* is a woven cloth on which designs are resist-dyed, or tie-dyed. Woven fabric comes in a variety of other forms. *Pha khit* is usually woven from cotton and used mainly for blankets, shawls and mats on which monks sit. These are made primarily in northeastern Thailand, although some of the central and northern provinces also produce *pha khit*. *Pha jok* is a delicate decorative weave used on its own or to embellish traditional mats and triangular cushions. In *pha yok*, gold and silver threads are woven into the fabric for a gorgeous lustre.

Northern hill tribe textiles are traditionally embroidered or appliquéd, and dyed using natural colours. Traditional tribal Akha pieces are cross-stitched using shades of pinks and blues. Hmong pieces are batiked using indigo and have cross-stitched borders predominantly in yellow, orange and white. Woven cottons in dark blue or black are used as background palettes for the intricate fabric work.

Pottery and Ceramics

The craft of pottery has a long history in Thailand. Since prehistoric times, glazed and unglazed pottery have been used for food and water storage as well as for decoration. Baan Chiang Pottery dating from about 5600 BC was found in Udon Thani Province. Designs in a distinctive red pigment were etched, drawn or delicately cut into the Baan Chiang artifacts, which included jars, vases, sculptures and beads.

Today, Thai pottery is made from ball clay and white clay. Ball clay is black and common throughout the country. To stabilise the clay and prevent it from cracking or losing its shape, baked clay is added to the unbaked clay before shaping and firing. White clay produces a white product after firing. It is of a higher quality because it contains minerals such as feldspar. It is typically found in northern Thailand in Lampang Province but also in the southern provinces of Ranong and Surat Thani.

Ancient Ceramics

Ceramics, especially Sangkhalok ware, were an important art form of the Sukhothai period. Kilns just outside the city of Sukhothai produced monochrome white-glazed and underglazed black pieces. Other kilns in the Sukhothai kingdom produced monochrome brown-glazed pieces and ceramics in other colours. Sangkhalok Ware was very popular and was exported to Indonesia, the Philippines and elsewhere in Southeast Asia. Today, many of these pieces can be viewed in museums in Thailand and other parts of Southeast Asia.

Celadon

Celadon was introduced into Thailand during the Sukhothai Era, probably owing to Chinese influence. The remnants of large kilns have been found in Sukothai Province. Celadon comes from the Sanskrit words *sila* (stone) and *dhara* (green). Celadon was used in temple decorations and for Buddhist and Hindu mythological figures and sculptures.

During the 15th century, when China began to isolate itself from the outside world, Thai celadon became coveted and major production began in Chiang Mai. When the Burmese invaded Siam in the mid-16th century, Siamese celadon artisans were captured and taken to Burma. The art returned to the Chiang Mai area from the late 18th century onwards, as celadon artisans migrated to Thailand from troubled areas in Burma.

Today's kilns are modelled after the ancient ones. Stoneware is fired at very high temperatures using a wood and ash glaze. The decorative cracks in the glaze are intentionally created as the glaze cools. The traditional colour of the glaze is green, but there are a wide variety of shades within that palette. Today authentic, traditional celadon pottery is made by hand, but machines and moulds are used for certain pieces, to keep up with the current high market demand for celadon.

There are several major producers of celadon in northern Thailand, including Baan Celadon and Siam Celadon in the Sankampaeng crafts area of Chiang Mai.

Benjarong Porcelain

Benjarong is a Thai porcelain that originated in 14th- to 17th-century China during the Ming Dynasty. Initially made only for royal and aristocratic use, it was traditionally created using five coloured enamels (red, white, yellow, black and green) on a white porcelain base. In the 18th century, bone ash was added to the porcelain, and the king's royal ceramicists were sent to England to learn the techniques of adding bone and special clays, resulting in the Royal Benjarong, known for the exceptional quality of its glaze and translucency. In the 19th century, *lai nam thong*, or Benjarong with gold, became popular. The gold required a separate glazing. Many of the original pieces from this time are currently on display at the National Museum in

Bangkok. Today Benjarong can be owned and used by anyone and may have as few as three colours or as many as eight. Benjarong is produced primarily in Bangkok, Samut Sakhon and Lampang provinces. Genuine articles are painstakingly created in compliance with royal quality standards, using 18-carat gold and traditional Thai motifs such as animals, plants, and cultural symbols like the *garuda*. Imitation Benjarong pieces are very common and sometimes resemble the genuine articles very closely.

Other Pottery

Most markets sell vases and other household articles with decorative designs in blue on a white background. These pieces are made from a heavy clay containing silica, sand and flint. They are produced mainly in Ratchaburi, Nakhon Pathom, Chiang Mai and Bangkok. Dishes in a 'pineapple' design are produced in Lampang and available throughout the country.

Lacquerware

The 3,000-year-old craft of lacquerware probably came to northern Thailand from China. In the making of lacquerware products, objects of bamboo or wood are coated with a lacquer made from the resin of the *lac* tree (of the sumac family of plants, a family which also includes poison ivy). The tree grows in northern Thailand and parts of central and southern China. It is tapped for its sap, which is purified by heating. A clear lacquer is made by adding a solvent to the mixture. The lacquer is applied to the object in several coats, each of which must be left to dry before another coat is added. Finally, a design is painted on the surface. Finished lacquerware has a beautiful sheen and is very durable, resisting water, heat and humidity.

There are several varieties of lacquerware, designated by their method of production. In the Ancient method, pigment was simply applied to the finished article. Later, *lac* and charcoal powder were mixed and applied in threads to the design, along with gold leaf. Pearl-inlaid lacquerware was once only for the king and the upper echelons of Thai society. Small pieces of pearl were embedded in the lacquer resin. The small pieces were placed under layer upon layer of lacquer. Today, the process usually involves glueing the mother-of-pearl directly onto the surface of the lacquered object. Similarly, one method of producing gold-overlaid lacquerware is by applying the gold leaf directly onto the lacquered item. Embedding pieces of glass in the resin was originally reserved for theatrical items. Today picture frames, boxes and even sculptures are made using this process. Chiang Mai Province is renowned for its production of lacquerware.

GILDED LACQUERWARE

Northern Thailand is known for its gilded black lacquerware. Gilded lacquerware was at its peak during the Ayutthaya Period and in Bangkok from the mid-17th to the end of the 18th centuries. The lacquer surface is polished and then the gold leaf is painted on in a similar resist method to that used in batik. The design is usually first drawn on paper, then placed over its intended area on the lacquer. Small pinpricks of gold leaf are made through the paper onto the object, and ash or chalk is pressed over the dots. A resist is applied to the areas meant to remain clear, and then the entire surface is coated with a quick-drying lacquer resin. Then all is washed with water, and the gold leaf remains on the design lines, while the rest of the object is coated in the clear lacquer.

Handmade Paper

Papermaking probably originated in China. Records of papermaking in Thailand can be traced back about 700 years. Paper was used for Buddhist texts and temple writings. Originally it was made from the inner bark of the *khoi* tree, or Siamese rough bush, a medium-sized tree with small, dense leaves. Today it is also made from the inner bark of the mulberry tree, or *sa*, which is much more common in Thailand and grows naturally in the northern forests.

Handmade paper is made in Thailand by shredding the material used and then soaking it overnight so that the fibres loosen. The fibres are boiled for two to six hours, after which they are washed with clean water and the impurities removed, usually by hand. The fibres are then beaten by hand or machine until they resemble a smooth pulp. Dyes can be added at this time, and the pulp is then put into a large tub. A framed screen is dipped into the water to catch the fibres. Then the screen is put out into the sun to dry. The paper can then be shifted to boards, pressed, smoothed and dried. It is used to make notebooks, diaries and notecards. It is also stretched over bamboo frames to make traditional kites and umbrellas.

Woodcarving

The discovery of prehistoric utensils with wooden handles suggests that wood has been used for thousands of years in Thailand. The country's softwood trees grow in the mountains of the north, while teak and rubber are found in forests throughout Thailand. Woodcarving is a valued art in Thailand, with a history dating back at least to the Sukhothai period.

Decorative items such as picture carvings in both sculpture and bas-relief feature Buddhist legends, historical events and rural life. These pieces are made in the provinces of Chiang Mai, Sukhothai, Phitsanulok, Nan, Prae, Lampang, Lampoon and Mae Hong Son. Ornamental carvings to adorn traditional Thai architecture are usually made in Bangkok and Chiang Mai provinces. Thai wood furniture is very distinctive. Many pieces reveal Chinese influence, especially in the shape and design of the carvings. Woodcarvings are also used to decorate royal furniture.

Basket-Making

The earliest mention of baskets dates from the Sukhothai period, when they were used for carrying water. These baskets were made from bamboo and rattan, with the final product caulked to prevent water from leaking.

Today bamboo and rattan are the main materials used for making baskets in Thailand. Bamboo is found naturally in Thailand and used for many different kinds of items. Rattan makes more durable baskets than bamboo. A member of the palmae family, the rattan plant is found in the southern provinces of Surat Thani, Songkhla, Ranong, Krabi and Pattani.

Baskets have many uses—as animal traps, containers, for numerous other household uses and for decoration. Broad open baskets are used for carrying fruits and vegetables. A *kradong* is a round, flattish tray with a relatively close weave used for winnowing or drying seeds or other items.

A *takraeng* is a round, loosely woven flat tray used as a sieve. A *kraboong* is a basket with three or four leg extensions. In the past it was used mostly to measure grains, but nowadays it is used for just about any purpose. A *khlong khao* is a container used for cooked "sticky" rice. Fish traps are long cylindrical containers either used vertically or horizontally. Chicken coops are dome-shaped and are sold at small basket kiosks by the roadside.

Thai Dolls

Dolls produced in Thailand include theatrical dolls that represent the characters of the *Ramakien*, period dolls representing Thai life in different historical eras and hill tribe dolls representing the traditional costumes of the northern hill tribe groups. Materials used include clay, cloth, wood, plastic and paper. The most famous stuffed dolls, Bangkok Dolls, are handmade by award-winning doll-maker Khunying Tongkorn Chandavimol and her team of about 20 doll-makers.

METAL CRAFT

Bronze

Known as *thong samrid* in Thai, bronze is an alloy of copper and tin. Buddha images have been made of bronze for hundreds of years. Bronze does not contain lead and can be used safely around food and food products. Very popular are bronze utensils, dishes and cutlery sets. Bronze ware is produced primarily in Bangkok, Ayutthaya and Samutprakam provinces.

Gold

During the Ayutthaya period, pure gold was used for Buddha images, royal ceremonial objects and gold leaf. Prior to 1957, some of Thailand's richest troves of gold were in the crypt of the 15th-century tower of Wat Ratchaburana in Ayutthaya. Although thieves stole most of it in 1957, about 2,000 pieces were retrieved and are now on display at the Chao Sam Phraya National Museum in Ayutthaya.

The making of gold jewellery probably began with the Khmer at Sukhothai. The engraved blocks found at Wat Si Chum in Sukhothai feature characters from *The Jataka Tales* decorated with gold jewellery, including necklaces and crowns. Over the centuries, demand for gold jewellery has remained steady among the wealthy, and today Thailand's gold production centres are Bangkok, Chiang Mai and Sukhothai provinces.

Silver

The silver alloy used for decorative articles in Bangkok is at least 95-per cent silver, with copper usually making up the remaining part. The hill tribes of northern Thailand emboss beautiful designs onto jewellery and decorative items. The artisans of northern Thailand employ anaglyph, the process of carving designs in low relief.

Nielloware is a special decorative art process created on silver, silver/gold and gold. Beautiful designs are drawn or screened onto the object and then delicately carved either by hand or by special machine. A mixture of metals (sulphides of lead, copper and silver) is applied to the carved areas and combined with a soldering substance. Heat is applied so that the amalgam dissolves and sticks to the object, creating opaque blackened areas. When cooled and dry, the object is sanded and then polished either by hand or by machine.

Nielloware objects may take several months to complete, with larger pieces often made only by commission. Bowls, jewellery, tea and coffee sets and purses are some examples of items created using this art form. For centuries Nielloware has been offered to kings and foreign dignitaries as a special and prestigious gift.

Gemstone Jewellery

Many kinds of gemstones are found in Thailand, including diamond, ruby, blue sapphire, aquamarine, spinel, garnet, onyx, yellow sapphire, zircon, amethyst, rose quartz, peridot, opal, pearl, bloodstone and agate. Rubies and sapphires are found in Chanthaburi and Trat province. Some blue sapphires are found in Kanchanaburi province. The provinces of Phrae, Sukhothai, Petchaburi,

Ubon Ratchathani and Si Sa Ket produce many gemstones. Pearl is cultured in the southern provinces of Phuket, Phang-Nga and Ranong.

In Thailand many people believe that certain gemstones possess supernatural powers, particularly diamond, ruby, emerald, yellow sapphire, garnet, onyx, moonstone, zircon and chrysoberyl. Jewellery decorated with these gemstones is popular; it is believed that cumulatively the gemstones have the power to bring increased good fortune. The most popular settings for gemstones are gold and silver.

OTOP

One Tambon One Product, or OTOP, was launched in Thailand in 2001 to encourage local craft and industry through the manufacture and marketing of traditional products. The brainchild of the former governor of Oita Prefecture in Japan, Morihiko Hiramatsu, OTOP aims to help local communities increase their financial resources and nurture pride in the communities. The concept was very successful in Japan and spread to other cities and countries worldwide, including Thailand.

The *tambon*, or village, is the local Thai administrative unit, and OTOP aspires to allow people to remain in their communities while using their handicraft skills. The government assists in development and marketing, thus generating jobs, income and community growth. In central Thailand, products are made using flax, reeds, bamboo, forest vines, water hyacinth fibres and palm leaves. Northern Thailand produces carved wood products, hill tribe textiles, handmade paper and jewellery. Southern Thailand is known for artificial flowers and woven products made from local plants such as the pandanus (a plant with flat, blade-like fragrant leaves) and lipao (a tropical vine). Northeastern Thailand produces specialty woven cloth and Dan Gwian pottery, a unique type of pottery known for its rough texture and brownish red colour.

THE THAI
CALENDAR

The Thai calendar takes as its reference point Lord Buddha's death 543 years before Jesus Christ. Therefore year 1 of the Thai Buddhist Era, BE 1, corresponds to the year 543 BC in the Western calendar.

THE THAI LUNAR CALENDAR

The Thai lunar calendar is called the Chantarakti. Each lunar cycle lasts 29 days, 12 hours and 44 minutes. The month begins at the start of the new moon. The full moon marks the middle of the month and is called Wan Kuen Sib Ha Kham. The last day of the month is called either Wan Ram 15 Kham or Wan Ram 14 Kham, depending on whether the month has 30 or 29 days. The months are numbered from one to twelve: *ai* (one), *yi* (two), *sam* (three), *si* (four), *ha* (five), *hok* (six), *jed* (seven), *pad* (eight), *kao* (nine), *sib* (ten), *sib-ed* (eleven) and *sib-song* (twelve).

The Thai calendar year is about twelve days shorter than the Western (solar) calendar year. To compensate, every two or three years the eighth month is doubled. This second, extra eighth month is called Duen Pad Lung. A year with two eighth months is called Athikamas. To compensate for missing days, every four or five years an extra day is added to the seventh month, making it a 30-day month. This day, the Athikawara, is never added in an Athikamas year.

OTHER CALENDARS

The Chinese Calendar

The Chinese (lunar) calendar is well known throughout Thailand, and Chinese New Year is widely celebrated. The Chinese calendar consists of 12-year cycles in which each year is denoted by an animal. The twelve animals of the Chinese zodiac are the *chuad* (rat), *chalu* (bull), *khal* (tiger), *toa* (hare), *maroang* (dragon), *maseng* (snake), *mamia* (horse), *mamaae* (goat), *wog* (monkey), *raga* (rooster), *jau* (dog) and *goon* (pig). The year 2007 was the Year of the Pig, and 2008 is the Year of the Rat.

The Western Calendar

The Western calendar is based on a solar year, or the time it takes for the Earth to circle the sun. A solar year lasts 365 days, 5 hours, 48 minutes and 45.68 seconds. The year is divided into months that have 28, 29 (in leap years), 30 or 31 days.

HOLIDAYS AND FESTIVALS

Chinese New Year

The Chinese New Year is calculated according to the lunar calendar and usually falls in January or February. In preparation for the start of the new lunar year, people clean their homes and go to the markets to buy food and special offerings. Chinese businesses and stalls close for the holiday period.

On New Year's Eve, many Chinese families celebrate with a 'reunion' dinner, usually hosted by the most senior patriarch or matriarch, that brings together all the family members.

On New Year's Day, many Chinese people rise early to put on new clothes and visit their local temples to pray and make offerings to ancestors and gods. Then they celebrate the New Year by visiting family and friends and exchanging blessings and oranges, which represent good fortune. Children receive *ang pao*—red packets containing gifts of money that symbolise prosperity and good fortune.

Parades are held in Bangkok's Chinatown and other parts of Thailand where there are large populations of Chinese people. The evening skies are ablaze with fireworks and firecrackers.

Chakri Day

The founding of the Chakri Dynasty is commemorated on 6 April. The dynasty began with Rama I, who became the king of Thailand on 6 April 1782. As of 2007, there have been nine kings of the Chakri Dynasty, including King Bhumibol Adulyadej, who reigns as Rama IX.

Chakri Day is a time for the royal family and the Thai people to honour the kings of Thailand. The royal family officiates a religious ceremony at the Royal Chapel to give merit to the past rulers. This is followed by a visit to the Royal Pantheon, which houses life-sized statues of the kings of the Chakri Dynasty. The procession proceeds to Memorial Bridge, where a wreath is placed on the statue of King Rama I.

Songkran

The traditional Thai New Year, Songkran, is celebrated from 13 April to 15 April. Its date used to vary according to astrological calculations but is now fixed.

During Songkran, small shops and businesses close and people leave the cities to return to their home villages and towns to spend the holidays with their families. It is a time for Thais to make sure their homes are clean, show kindness and consideration to parents and the elderly and pay their respects to Buddha images at the temples. Songkran falls during the hottest time of the year, and Songkran is also known as the Water Festival because one of the holiday's most enjoyed and best-known customs is the dousing of people with water. This practice is in fact derived from the pouring of scented waters over the hands of parents and the elderly as a mark of respect.

Songkran is also a time for merit-making, and people bring food for the monks at the local temples. Another merit-making gesture is the showing of kindness to animals. People seek out caged animals and fish accidentally trapped in waterways too small, releasing them into freer environments.

The Royal Ploughing Ceremony

Originating in ancient India before the birth of Lord Buddha, the Royal Ploughing Ceremony marks the beginning of the planting season at the start of the rainy period, when rice is sown. The annual ceremony usually happens in May, but the date is not fixed because it is determined each year by the royal astrologers.

Held in Bangkok at Sanam Luang near the Grand Palace, the Royal Ploughing Ceremony involves the blessing of rice grains at the Temple of the Emerald Buddha. Brahmin priests oversee the ploughing of the ceremonial rice beds and the planting of the rice. At the conclusion of the ceremony, the priests predict the season's rainfall and yield based on the length of cloth selected from among three options—a long piece indicating little rain, a medium piece indicating average rain and a short piece indicating an abundant rainfall. After ploughing is completed, onlookers run into the fields to gather up rice seeds believed to be a token of good fortune. They mix these with their own rice seeds to ensure a good harvest.

Coronation Day

This holiday is observed on 5 May and commemorates the day in 1950 when His Majesty King Bhumibol Adulyadej the Great was crowned king of Thailand. Festivities begin on 3 May with a merit-making ceremony dedicated to deceased kings. On 4 May the Chief Brahmin Priest reads the Proclamation of Coronation Day, and on 5 May there is a 21-gun salute by the army and navy, after which the king presents royal decorations.

Loy Krathong and Yee Peng

One of the most beautiful festive sights, the Loy Krathong celebration takes place on the evening of the full moon in November. It is said that the festival originated in India to thank the goddess of water. The word *loy* means "to float", and a *krathong* is a small 'boat' made from banana leaves. Candles, sticks of incense, flowers and money are placed in the small boat. At moonlight, the candles and incense in the *krathong* are lit, a wish is made and the boats are cast into the water to drift until they disappear from sight. People float *krathong* for many reasons: to seek blessings from the goddess of water, to ward off bad fortune, even to ask for a sign. For instance it is said that if two lovers launch a *krathong* together and the candle on the vessel stays lit against the elements, it is a sign that their love will be everlasting.

In the northern city of Chiang Mai, the full moon in November is celebrated the evening before and known as Yee Peng. The festival has a religious emphasis and is a time of merit-making. Instead of sending boats down waterways, lanterns called *khom loy* are made by covering bamboo frames with sheets of mulberry paper. A torch is lit within the lantern and it is launched into the evening skies, borne by the wind. People believe that with the lantern go their misfortunes. Although lanterns are launched throughout northern Thailand during the Yee Peng festival, the Taepae Gate area in Chiang Mai has the most impressive display. So many lanterns fill the night sky there that the Royal Thai Air Force postpones all activities during this time, and commercial air traffic is warned to exercise caution.

The King's and Queen's Birthdays

Thailand's His Majesty King Bhumibol Adulyadej is the longest reigning monarch in Thai and world history. Born on 5 December 1927, he became King at the age of 19. He is greatly loved by Thai people everywhere for his warmth, political integrity and strong efforts to improve living conditions in rural areas. The King's birthday is a national holiday and a time of great celebration. The country is adorned with flags, banners, lights and large pictures of His Majesty the King, and people gather to bless their monarch with health, prosperity and fortitude.

Her Majesty Queen Sirikit was born on 12 August 1932. The daughter of the Thai ambassador to the United Kingdom, she was educated in Europe and met the monarch there. The Queen's birthday is celebrated as a public holiday and jointly as Mothers' Day, a time to honour mothers as Thais honour Her Majesty Queen Sirikit as the mother of the nation.

Constitution Day

An absolute monarchy ruled the kingdom of Thailand prior to 1932. On 24 June 1932, a constitutional monarchy was declared. Constitution Day is observed on 10 December. On this day buildings throughout the country are adorned with national flags, streamers, decorations and lights.

INTERNATIONAL
RELATIONS

The Thai system of government is a constitutional monarchy. Thais are proud of their long history of independence; the country has never been colonised by a European power. After a coup d'etat wrested power from the government of former prime minister Thaksin Shinawatra in September 2006, an interim constitution was put in place, with the promise of a new constitution to be declared in 2007. In December 2007 elections were held and the People's Power Party's Samak Sundaravej was declared the winner

Thailand has always appreciated foreign investment. Japan, Europe and North America are Thailand's major markets. Tourism is a significant industry in Thailand, accounting for about 6 per cent of Thailand's economy.

GOVERNMENT

The executive branch of government includes the king as the chief of state and the prime minister as the head of government. The legislative branch comprises the bicameral National Assembly (Rathasapha), made up of the 150-seat Senate (Wuthisapha) and the 480-seat House of Representatives (Sapha Phuthaen Ratsadon).

After the coup of September 2006, coup leaders appointed an interim National Assembly with 250 members to act as Senate and House of Representatives. The judicial branch of government consists of the Supreme

Court (Sandika), Constitutional Tribunal, Courts of Justice and administrative courts. There are 76 provinces that are further divided into districts, sub-districts, *tambon* and villages.

His Royal Majesty King Bhumibol Adulyadej (Rama IX) has been sovereign since 1946. He is highly revered by the Thai people. During his long and influential reign, he has participated in the resolution of numerous security issues that have threatened Thailand's stability.

FOREIGN RELATIONS

Relations with Japan

In September 2007, Thailand celebrated 120 years of diplomatic relations with Japan since signing the Declaration of Amity and Commerce in 1887. Special events and activities were scheduled to commemorate this event. The imperial family of Japan and the royal family of Thailand have a cordial relationship, and human resource exchanges between the two countries in fields such as politics and economics have been ongoing.

Relations with Australia

Thailand and Australia collaborate on areas of mutual interest including trade and investment, counter-terrorism, security, education and tourism. The Thailand-Australia Free Trade Agreement (TAFTA) has been in place since 2004, promoting two-way trade and business. Australia and Thailand have worked cooperatively in the World Trade Organization (WTO) and Asia-Pacific Economic Cooperation (APEC), an inter-governmental forum facilitating economic growth, cooperation, trade and investment in the Asia-Pacific region.

Relations with the United States

Thailand has maintained a close relationship with the United States since World War II. In 2004, the United States and Thailand commenced negotiations on a free trade agreement between the two countries. The discussions were temporarily halted following the suspension of the Thai parliament in February 2006 and the September 2006 coup d'etat. Thailand was one of the eight countries (United States, Australia, New Zealand, The Philippines, Pakistan, Thailand, Britain and France) that signed the Manila Pact of the former Southeast Asia Treaty Organization in 1954. Even though SEATO was dissolved in 1977, the Manila Pact continues to be valid. The US government continues to work with Thailand in areas where both agree there is a need, including refugee assistance and curbing illicit drug trafficking. The US Peace Corps has approximately 100 volunteers serving in Thailand in primary and teacher education and community development.

Relations with the European Union

The European Union (EU) and Thailand concentrate on a relationship of mutual cooperation rather than development assistance that includes economic issues, higher education, science and technology and human rights. In 2005, the European Union was ASEAN's third largest trading partner after the United States and Japan.

PARTICIPATION IN INTERNATIONAL ORGANISATIONS

The Association of Southeast Asian Nations (ASEAN)

Thailand is an active member and one of the five founding members (Thailand, Indonesia, Malaysia, The Philippines and Singapore) of the Association of Southeast Asian Nations (ASEAN). Founded in 1967, ASEAN now includes four additional member countries (Brunei Darussalam, Vietnam, Lao People's Democratic Republic, Myanmar and Cambodia). ASEAN is committed to achieving economic, social and cultural goals using through joint efforts, active collaboration and mutual assistance. Thailand has also participated in the Organization of American States (OAS), and the Organization for Security and Cooperation in Europe (OSCE).

The United Nations (UN)

Thailand strongly supports the activities and organisation of the United Nations (UN). It has contributed troops to international peacekeeping forces and has been a proponent for human rights and environmental concerns and treaties. Several regional UN organisations have representative offices in Bangkok, including the UN Economic and Social Commission for Asia and the Pacific (UNESCAP) and the regional centre of the UN Development Program. More than 20 related UN agencies are operating within Thailand. The United Nations complex is located in Bangkok.

The United Nations plays a role in Thailand's overall development process and was also closely involved in responding to the tsunami crisis of 2004. The UN provided relief assistance and recovery, assisting in the tsunami's impact on the environment, fishing and tourism and other industries.

OTHER CONCERNS

The Tsunami Crisis of 2004

The tsunami of 2004 was the worst natural disaster ever to strike Thailand, causing loss of life as well as major damage to property, the environment and the economy. Beginning with an earthquake off the coast of Sumatra, the catastrophic event concluded with more than 5,300 people killed and over 2,800 missing. More than 4,800 houses were destroyed or damaged. The estimated (not including housing) damage was more than US$ 350 million. Thailand bore a significant amount of the reconstruction costs itself. However, millions of dollars were donated from international agencies and the global community.

Ongoing national and international efforts continue in areas such as disaster preparedness and the protection of vulnerable groups (especially migrant workers and sea gypsies) and children. Local communities and authorities continue to need assistance in the areas of child welfare, livelihood restoration, tourism and psychological impact.

Avian and Human Influenza

Since human cases of avian influenza became a critical concern in Southeast Asia in 2004 and 2005, the United Nations and the World Health Organization (WHO) have both been closely involved in working with Thailand on prevention, surveillance and monitoring. The WHO and the US Centers for Disease Control have worked closely with the Thai government, offering regional and local workshops; policy and prevention; and strategic planning and education on avian influenza.

THAI PERSONAGES

KING CHULALONGKORN

Becoming king in 1868 when he was just 15 years old, King Chulalongkorn is known for his ardent support for education and for his tempered acceptance and integration of Western influences. His diplomatic skill and political knowledge helped preserve Thai independence in the face of threats of European colonisation.

King Chulalongkorn reigned for 42 years. Among his many achievements were the founding of a Western-style government that paved the way for democracy; the establishment of the country's first hospital and medical school based on Western medicine; and the implementation of a nationwide education system. King Chulalongkorn remains one of Thailand's best-loved monarchs.

KING BHUMIBOL ADULYADEJ

Born in Cambridge, Massachusetts in 1927 while his father was studying at Harvard University, His Majesty King Bhumibol Adulyadej (King Rama IX) has served as the King of Thailand since 1950. An inventive scientist, gifted linguist and accomplished musician, composer and poet, the monarch is a multi-talented and exceptional sovereign loved and revered by the Thai people. His Majesty The King is committed to improving the lives of the Thai people and has been active in promoting the development of health care for rural regions. Free clinics and mobile health care units have been created for the rural, the poor and people living in remote areas. Along with his wife, His Majesty King Bhumibol Adulyadej has established research and other foundations to help people suffering from cholera, polio, tuberculosis, leprosy and other chronic diseases. Education is another strong interest, and through his Distance Learning Foundation, both vocational and university education have reached rural populations. Profoundly interested in agriculture, the monarch continues to fund projects assisting rural people in improving agricultural techniques and construction. The royal couple are ardent supporters of Thai charities and pay frequent visits to rural communities.

SILPA BHIRASRI (CORRADO FEROCI)

Born in 1892 in Italy, Corrado Feroci studied art at the Royal Art Academy in Florence. He attained his qualifications as a professor, teaching in Italy until 1923 before arriving in Thailand at the invitation of the King Vajiravudh. Feroci is recognised for his valuable contribution to fine arts in Thailand.

Recognising the importance of contemporary art, the Thai government requested that Feroci design a curriculum to match the standard of European art schools, and he developed a Painting and Sculpture programme for the Royal Fine Arts Department in 1924. Feroci founded the School of Fine Arts in 1933, and the University of Fine Arts at Silpakorn University in 1943. From 1943 until his death in 1962 he was Professor and Dean at the Faculty of Painting and Sculpture. In 1944 he changed his name to Silpa Bhirasri and became a Thai national.

Silpha Bhirasri is considered the Father of Modern Arts in Thailand. Some of his best-known works include the statues of King Rama I (1929–1932), King Rama VI (1941), King Tak Sin the Great (1950–1951) and King Naresuan the Great in Suphan Buri Province (1956). He also modelled numerous famous monuments and statues throughout Thailand, including Democracy Monument, Victory Monument, and the design of the Walking Buddha (1955; cast in 1981) at Phutthamonthon just outside Bangkok. The Royal Government of Thailand presented him with the Most Notable Order of the Crown of Thailand and the Dusdi Mala Medal. He is the author of books and articles on both ancient and modern Thai art. His work and inspiration for Thai art and artists, combined with his passion for life, has left an indelible mark on Thailand. Silpa Bhirasri died in 1962. His birthday, 15 September, is commemorated as Silpa Bhirasri Day. The Silpa Bhirasri Memorial at the National Museum is dedicated to his memory.

MECHAI VIRAVAIDYA

Born in Australia in 1941 to a Scottish mother and Thai father who were both physicians, Mechai Viravaidya was raised to respect both Western and Thai cultural values and customs. He is recognised for his powerful contribution to public health in Thailand, in particular for raising HIV-awareness and prevention through public education.

Mechai Viravaidya graduated from the University of Melbourne in 1964 and got a job in Thailand with the National Economic and Social Development Board (NESDB). He gradually earned a newspaper and radio following for his reports and observations on economic and social development.

In the 1970s, Mechai revolutionised planned parenthood in Thailand. As founder of Community Based Family Planning Services (CBFPS), he and his team visited rural districts introducing family planning methods, information and assistance, enlisting the support of volunteers and government doctors in district centres. Contraceptives were offered at nominal costs and distributors received a small commission from the sales. In 1973 Mechai founded the Population and Community Development Association (PDA), a private organisation that continued his work in population control. In the 1980s, through creative marketing strategies and the frank dissemination of information, Mechai helped the country confront difficult issues like sexually transmitted diseases, HIV and AIDS at a time when such issues were often taboo and sufferers urgently needed support and understanding. Mechai's popularisation of condoms has earned him the nickname "Mr Condom", and condoms are sometimes called "mechais".

Today, with more than 800 staff members and over 12,000 volunteers in offices throughout Thailand, the PDA works at primary health care and

HIV/AIDS education and prevention, as well as water resource development and sanitation, environmental conservation, promotion of small-scale rural enterprise programmes, gender equality and youth development. The PDA is now also active in the rehabilitation of villages affected by the 2004 tsunami. The recipient of numerous international awards, the PDA recently earned the US$ 1-million 2007 Gates Award in recognition of global health. Presented by the Bill and Melinda Gates Foundation, the award is the world's largest prize for international health, dignifying extraordinary efforts directed at improving health in developing countries.

SURAYUD CHULANONT

Born the son of a former soldier in 1943, Surayud Chulanont was made Thailand's interim prime minister on 1 October 2006, following the coup d'etat of September 2006.

Surayud Chulanont revealed his leadership qualities during the insurgencies of the early 1990s, when as commander of the elite special forces he strongly condemned loss of life and lobbied to resolve situations without force. In 1997, he became commander-in-chief of the Thai army and worked to maintain ethical standards in the organisation. He was instrumental in responding quickly to allay threats along Thailand's borders, including illicit drug trafficking and risks to refugee camps. His stance towards Burmese refugees, especially the ethnic Karen, has been compassionate and fair.

Under his direction, the army participated in peacekeeping efforts in East Timor as well as in Aceh and Afghanistan. He is known for his important part in restoring the public image of Thailand's military. For his work and successes, human rights activists, defence analysts and military colleagues have lauded him. Surayud left the army in 2003, at which time he took the vows of temporary monkhood prior to becoming a senior consultant to the king.

Following the coup d'etat of September 2006, Surayud Chulanont was selected as the country's new prime minister for his reputation as a steadfast, morally upright and trustworthy leader.

SANGDUEN CHAILERT

Affectionately called the Elephant Whisperer, Sangduen Chailert is known for promoting the welfare of Asian elephants in Thailand. She was born in 1962 in a small hill tribe village north of Chiang Mai and grew up learning about healing from her grandfather, a shaman in northeastern Thailand. He once saved someone's life and was paid with an elephant that gradually became part of the family.

After graduating from Chiang Mai University, Sangduen started work in the elephant tourism industry. She observed a great deal of maltreatment and neglect of domestic Thai elephants and started to work towards improving their welfare. Today she runs the Elephant Nature Park and Elephant Haven, two elephant shelters in Chiang Mai province. At the Nature Park she works with a staff of elephant handlers, doctors and volunteers who nurse injured or abused elephants back to health. The elephants are then sent to Elephant Haven, where they can live safely in the forests until they die.

Sangduen was identified as a Hero of the Planet by *National Geographic* in 2001 and received two honorary degrees from Chiang Mai University. She was given the American Humane Society's Genesis Award in 2003 and named one of *Time Asia's* Heroes of the Year in 2005. The award-winning *National Geographic* documentary *Vanishing Giants* (2005) draws attention to her work. Sangduen Chailert now operates a mobile clinic for animals and continues to be active in promoting the humane treatment of elephants.

PARADON SRICHAPHAN

Born in 1979 in Bangkok, Paradorn Srichapan started playing tennis when he was six years old, coached by his father. He was tenth in the world junior rankings in 1996 and was a triple gold medalist (singles, doubles and team categories) at the Southeast Asia Games in Brunei in 1999.

In a competitive sport that requires focus, determination, commitment and ongoing self-assessment, Paradorn has succeeded in the international arena of tennis without surrendering his gentle and courteous qualities. Considered one of the world's best tennis players, he attained the rank of number 16 in the Association of Tennis Professionals (ATP) rankings in 2002 and is the first Asian male since 1980 to attain the status of being in the top 20. In 2002, he was also designated Thailand's cultural ambassador and named Thai of the Year. The following year he was chosen by *Time Asia* as one of its 29 Asian Heroes and was featured on the cover of the magazine.

JIM THOMPSON

Born in 1906, American entrepreneur Jim Thompson was educated at Princeton University and the University of Pennsylvania. During World War II he served in the US Army, undergoing demanding training in jungle survival. His group received assignments in North Africa, Italy, France and Asia. Thompson was on the way to Bangkok when the war ended. He turned his attention to helping refurbish the old Oriental Hotel in Bangkok. Later he became interested in the Thai silk industry, and in 1948 he joined with a group of Thai investors and founded the Thai Silk Company.

Silk-making was dying out as a household craft, and Thompson decided to revitalize the industry of handwoven silk. He identified a group of Cham (Muslim) weavers in Bangkok, obtained colourfast dyes and looms and provided technical assistance and support to weavers. Many in his workforce survived poverty because of the success of the silk industry and their ownership of shares in the Thai Silk Company. Many women were able to work from home, looking after their families while earning a living.

Jim Thompson was awarded the Order of the White Elephant for his role in renewing Thailand's silk industry. The award is presented to foreigners who offer exceptional service to Thailand. In 1967 Thompson mysteriously disappeared while holidaying in the Cameron Highlands in Malaysia. He went for an afternoon walk on Easter Sunday and never returned. His body was never found.

In 1976, a foundation in the name of Jim Thompson was established in Thailand. His house and art collection are now part of an officially registered museum site in Bangkok. The foundation is dedicated to the preservation and conservation of Thailand's cultural heritage.

TSUNAMI HEROES

Help International Phi Phi

One of the locations hardest hit by the tsunami of 26 December 2004 was Thailand's Phi Phi Islands. Businesses were destroyed and more than 700 people killed on these small islands. Thai authorities pronounced the islands uninhabitable. A group called Help International Phi Phi (Hi Phi Phi), consisting of foreign volunteers and Thais, was formed to help the islanders. Together the volunteers worked to feed and house the people who had lost their homes—hundreds of Thai refugees from Phi Phi living in temporary camps near Krabi. Hi Phi Phi also helped those who had lost loved ones identify and locate dead and missing persons.

Crisis Corps

US Peace Corps volunteers have served in Thailand since 1962, recently celebrating 45 years of service in Thailand. As an extension of this programme, in March 2005 in response to the tsunami that devastated southern Thailand, a group of eight Crisis Corps volunteers came to Thailand to assist in tsunami reconstruction in Thailand. The group included teachers, construction experts and lawyers, with skills and expertise ranging from database and resource development to building. They worked in cooperation with local communities to assess damage and costs for reconstruction of both structures and property. A second group of volunteers arrived in May 2005 expanding expertise to mental health, information technology and community development.

B I B L I O G R A P H Y

Amazing Thailand. (2000) Bangkok, Thailand: World Class Publishing

Asokananda & Harald B. (2004) *The Art of Traditional Thai Massage.*
Bangkok, Thailand: Editions Duang Kamol

Assumption University, Thailand. (2007) *Thai Arts and Literature 2/7/07.*
Retrieved from http://sunsite.au.ac.th/thailand/Thai_Arts/literature.html

Baker, C. & Phongpaicihit, P. (2005) *A History of Thailand.* Cambridge:
Cambridge University Press

Barang, M. (2006) *Thai Fiction in Translation.* Retrieved 10 August 2007
from http://www.thaifiction.com/english/list.html

Bradley, D.B. & Anderson, G.H. (1998) *Biographical Dictionary of Christian
Missions.* New York: Macmillan Reference USA; London: Simon &
Schuster and Prentice Hall International

Chadchaidee, T. (1994) *Essays on Thailand.* Bangkok, Thailand: D.K. Today
Co. Ltd.

Department of Health.(2004) *Global Statistics of Avian Influenza 20041027.*
Retrieved 9 June 2007 from World Organization for Animal Health
website: http://www.flu.org.cn/en/news-7248.html

Disayavanish, C. & Disayavanish, P. (December 1998) *Introduction of the Treatment Method of Thai Traditional Medicine: Its Validity and Future Perspectives*. Psychiatry Clinical Neuroscience. Suppl: S334-7

Encyclopedia Britannica. (2006) *Encyclopedia Britannica 2006 Ultimate Reference Suite*. [DVD]. England: Encyclopaedia Britannica (UK) Ltd

Gerson, R. (1996) *Traditional Festivals of Thailand*. Kuala Lumpur: Oxford University Press

A Golden Souvenir of the Culture, Tradition and Beliefs of Thailand. (2003) Bangkok, Thailand: Asia Books Co. Ltd.

Gompertz, G.S.G.M. (1960) *Celadon Wares*. London: Faber & Faber

Graham D.C. (1954) *Songs and Stories of the Ch'uan Miao.* Washington: Smithsonian Institution, Washington

Hoefer, H. (1995) *Insight Guides: Thailand.* Singapore: APA Publications

Holmes, H. & Suchada, T. (1997) *Working with Thais: A Guide to Managing in Thailand*. Bangkok, Thailand: White Lotus Co. Ltd.

Information Please Almanac Online. (2007). Retrieved on 6 June 2007 from http://www.infoplease.com/ipa/A0108034/html

Jumsai, M.L.M. (2002) *Thai Folktales: A Selection of the Gems of Thai Literature*. Bangkok, Thailand: Chalermnit

Lee, M.N.M. (1998) *The Thousand-Year Myth: Construction and Characterization of Hmong.* Hmong Studies Journal 2(2). Retrieved from http://hmongstudies.com/HSJ-v2n1_Lee.pdf

Lewis, P. & Lewis, E. (1984) *Peoples of the Golden Triangle*. Thailand: River Books

Masavisuth, Nitaya and Grose, Matthew. (1999) *S.E.A. Write Anthology of Thai Short Stories and Poems*. Bangkok, Thailand: Silkworm Books

McGraw, A. *Thai Music from National Geographic*. Retrieved on 15 June 2007 from http://worldmusic.nationalgeographic.com/worldmusic/ view/page.basic/genre/content.genre/thai_classical_music

Ministry of Industry. (1999) *Thai Handicraft Products*. Bangkok, Thailand: Ministry of Industry

Mollman, S. (2007) Sepak Takraw Grows by Leaps and Bounds. *Time*. Retrieved 5 August 2007 from http://www.time.com/time/magazine/ article/0,9171,1622158,00.html

National Museum Volunteers. (1996) *Writing from Asia: Treasures, Myths and Traditions*. Thailand: National Museum Volunteers

Pluvier, J.M. (1995) *Historical Atlas of Southeast Asia*. Leiden: E.J. Brill

Senawong, P. (2006) *Thai Ties: Social Customs and Cultural Traits that Tie All Thais*. Thailand: Silpakorn University

Sriparam, Chami/Southeast Asia Site/Northern Illinois University. (2007) *Thai Classical Music*. Retrieved 1 July 2007. http://www.seasite.niu.edu/

Sthapitanonda, N. & Mertens B. (2005) *Architecture of Thailand: A Guide to Traditional and Contemporary Forms*. Singapore: Editions Didier Millet

The Story of Ramakian, English translation (2002) Bangkok, Thailand: Sangdad Pueandek Publishing Co. Ltd.

Sunthorn, P. (2001) *Nirat Muang Klaeng*. Translated by Prem Chaya (H.H. Prince Prem Purachatra). Edited by Montri Umavijani. Kurusapa Business Organization

Surintatiip, D.S. (1999) *Have Fun with Thai Proverbs*. Bangkok, Thailand: R 3 K Company Limited

The Temple of the Emerald Buddha and the Grand Palace, English translation (2002) Bangkok, Thailand: Sangdad Pueandek Publishing Co. Ltd.

Thai Baht Gains Value, Thailand Loses Exports. (2007) Retrieved on
 29 August 2007 from Asia Economic Institute, Vol 1, No 5.
 website: www.asiecon.org

Thailand Timeline: A Chronology of Key Events. (2007) Retrieved 29 August
 2007 from BBC website: http://news.bbc.co.uk/1/hi/world/
 asia-pacific/country_profiles/1243059.stm

Toth, M.D. (1971) *Tales from Thailand.* Rutland: Tuttle

Velder, C. and Katrin A. (2003) *The Rice Birds: Folktales from Thailand.*
 Bangkok, Thailand: White Lotus Co. Ltd

Virulak, Suraphone. (1980) *Likay: A Popular Theatre in Thailand.* Unpublished
 doctoral dissertation, University of Hawaii, Honolulu

Wells, M.B. (1964) *Thai Fairy Tales.* Bangkok, Thailand: Church of Christ in
 Bangkok

Wong, C. (2002) 7th Thailand International Kite Festival. *Kitelife Magazine
 Issue 27* (Summer 2002). Retrieved 27 June 2007 from
 http://www.kitelife.com/archives summer02/thailand_festival.htm46
 http://www.thaikite.com/competition.html

Wyatt, D.K. (2003) *Thailand: A Short History.* Chiang Mai,
 Thailand: Silkworm Books

A U T H O R

ELLEN LONDON was born and raised in New York City. She is an accomplished musician, and holds a graduate degree in Librarianship from the University of Washington. For the past 30 years, she and her husband have worked and lived in Africa (Lesotho, Kenya, Ethiopia, Morocco), France, and Asia (Bangladesh, Thailand). For 20 years, she worked with international schools providing group and individual workshops on research and information retrieval to librarians, teachers and students, as well as presenting at international conferences. Ellen is the author of the book, *Countries of the World: Bangladesh* and numerous print and electronic articles on librarianship, storytelling and electronic information. She was the recipient of a Whitney-Carnegie Grant from the American Library Association as well as a Fulbright Scholarship. She is currently the director for Creative Design and Development for Firefly Designs Africa * Asia. Ellen and her husband Rit live and work in Thailand, and divide their time between their permanent residences in the United States and France. They have two grown daughters living in Louisiana and Virginia in the United States.

ACKNOWLEDGEMENTS

The author would like to thank Mr. Ekkarin Latthasaksiri (Librarian) of the Siam Society, and Maria Laosunthara (Thai Library Association) for their help in locating and identifying resources for this book's research.

INDEX